Finally, a provocative, breakthrough novelty in organizational design predestined to leave a mark in the field of Organizational Development.

Georg Schroeckenfuchs, CEO, Novartis Italia

An important contribution to our understanding of the structural changes necessary to promote organizational collaboration and innovation. Highly recommended.

Michael J. Gelb, author of How to Think Like Leonardo da Vinci and Innovate Like Edison

Self-directed and governing organizations have long been imagined but not fully realized because of the inherent problems with imposing structure on existing systems. AEquacy provides the radical yet practical, scalable, and inspirational solution to this problem. The book is well researched, using current interviews with CEOs and thought leaders as well as important studies from qualified researchers. Read and apply this book if you want your organization to emerge from the suffocation caused by hierarchy to the breathing space of an open system with free-flowing ideas, information, and integrated processes. You will discover new capacities, fresh energy, and results beyond your expectations.

Marcia Reynolds, Author of: Outsmart Your Brain, Wander Woman, and The Discomfort Zone: How Leaders Turn Difficult Conversations into Breakthroughs

AEQUACY.

A NEW HUMAN-CENTERED ORGANIZATIONAL DESIGN TO THRIVE IN A COMPLEX WORLD.

GIOVANNA D'ALESSIO - STEFANO PETTI

Published in 2018

First printing: 2018

ISBN n. 9788890957642

Publishing company:
Asterys s.r.l.
Via di Villa Zingone, 36
Rome, Italy 00151

www.asterys.com

"You never change things by fighting the existing reality. To change something, build a new model that makes the existing model obsolete."

Richard Buckminster Fuller

CONTENTS

ACKNOWLEDGMENTS

Many great thinkers influenced our research project and shaped the values and mindset that brought us to conceive AEquacy. Among those we would like to mention Barry Oshry, whose work on typical organizational dynamics was for us eye-opening; Peter Senge, who popularized system thinking in an organizational setting; Fritjof Capra, who offered us a new vision of the organization as a living system; Frederic Laloux, who linked organizational evolution to the theory of Spiral Dynamics and introduced the concept of Teal organization; Betty Cadbury and Kees Boeke, followed by Gerard Endenburg, who developed Sociocracy and paved the way to one of the biggest shifts in the management paradigm; Brian Robertson, who created the organizational system known as Holacracy and was the pioneer in structuring organizations as networks of self-managed teams.

We owe our gratitude to the CEOs and executives who were patient enough to be subject to our hailstorm of questions during the research interviews: Philippe Barrois, Arrigo Berni, Phil Clotier, Paola Corna Pellegrini, Giglio del Borgo, Laura Donnini, Miles

Graham, Søren Hagh, Donato Iacovone, Hugh O'Byrne, Guido Meardi, Magda Mook, Emmanuel Mottrie, and Georg Schroeckenfuchs. A special thank you goes to the Executives who first tested the AEquacy idea: Sertac Yeltekin, Simona Liguoro, Marco Bonaguidi, and Giglio del Borgo again.

We want to extend our heartfelt thank you to our editors Penelope Krumm and Barbara Sgarzi. Without their language mastery and attention to detail, this book would have never been the same.

Our deep appreciation goes to Cristina Bruni. Without her support, kindness and dedication to Asterys, its associates and its clients, we would have never been able to find the time to write the book.

Finally, we want to acknowledge our life partners, Pier Paolo Colasanti and Vendela Wikberg, for always being patient and loving, even when we spent hours on our keyboards during our vacations. This book is dedicated to them.

FOREWORD

Looking for a new organizational model; one that brings agility and engagement to the workplace, then you need look no further than the AEquacy approach. Based on decades of experience, Giovanna D'Alessio and Stefano Petti of Asterys, bring forward a new model of business organization; one that creates a culture of true collaboration, boosts performance and unleashes the potential of all employees.

At the core of their approach are the following ideas: self-organization, the organization as a living system, human equality and transparency. An aequal organization transcends the dysfunctions that inevitably come with hierarchy and that hinder performance, such as internal competition, silos, lack of collaboration, risk-aversion, control and micro-management.

The creation of a shared purpose and set of values allows for a stronger employee alignment and a unified compass for decision-making; The possibility for people to self-organize and coordinate ignites people with empowerment and sense of accountability; The simplification of processes and policies makes room for greater agility; The removal of subordination and of the boundaries between teams and departments boosts collaboration.

A fundamental requirement of this type of organization is trust. Working in an organization that embraces trust, is an invitation to personal development—leaving behind the fears of the ego to embrace the desires of the soul.

Every soul has three fundamental desires—to self-express, connect and contribute. The ego translates these desires into goals—finding meaning and purpose, making a difference and service. This is the energy our workplaces need to tap into; the energy that our workplaces are looking for. The Aequacy approach creates workplaces that while supporting employees on this journey, drives innovation and performance.

Richard Barrett
Chairman and Founder of the Barrett Values Centre.

1 - OUR JOURNEY FROM HIERARCHY TO AEQUACY

A wake-up call

In 2016 a study by Deloitte grabbed our attention. Deloitte's "The New Organization: Different by Design" survey of 7,000 respondents in more than 130 countries showed very interesting results: 82% of large companies are either currently reorganizing, plan to reorganize, or have recently reorganized to be more responsive to customer needs; 92% of the companies surveyed cite "redesigning the way we work" as one of their key challenges, making this the #1 trend or concern of the year; 90% of companies cite leadership as a major problem, and nearly 2/3 of all respondents rate that problem as "urgent".

Respondents say that the leaders they need today must be agile, they must learn rapidly, and they must be connected throughout the organization; only 19% of the sample believe they have the "right culture".

Of course we were well aware that many organizations were going through their umpteenth re-organization and that many had issues surrounding leadership and culture, but these numbers really struck us. Were these issues so pervasive? How could we help clients to be in better organizational, cultural, and structural shape to not just survive, but thrive in the next 10 years?

Statistics from these survey indicate that reorganization, leadership & culture are major org. problems

Do you really think your challenges are unique?

Large organizations have been facing increasingly complex challenges in the last thirty years. More and more often we have listened to a number of corporate leaders sharing their concerns about issues that hinder their organizational performance and their employees' accountability and engagement.

examples

"*When we concern ourselves exclusively with the control dimension, we create red tape: bureaucracy. And bureaucracy becomes an element that gets in the way of the final result.*" Giglio del Borgo, Managing Director of Diners Club Italia is sure about that. He continues: "*Processes are thought to ensure the existence of centers of control and to channel how people perform their job in an adequate and predictable fashion. But we should ask ourselves if the organizational structure, and the processes that go with it, reflect the best way to serve the customers, because these two elements are not always aligned. Sometimes we focus on creating a process to put risk under control without considering what the outcome is for the customer, how it translates into an experience that the customer can consider positive.*"

One of the worries of Hugh O'Byrne, former VP Global Sales Center Excellence, Digital Business Group at IBM Europe, is how to attract millennials: "*Millennials want to be more engaged but we are still working with a Victorian command & control style. The idea of command & control is losing some relevance and we're not fast enough anyway. We may need to move toward giving people more freedom.*"

"*Flexibility is a big challenge. To be extreme, in the future there would be no more organizational structure. We need to de-structure to be flexible and this is a challenge,*" noted Philippe Barrois, former CEO of Novartis France. "*Structure is comfortable. You are the boss, you have a team and this a way to feel protected and be in the comfort zone.*"

A silo mentality, a reductionist approach where work is fragmented, a rigid structure, stultifying bureaucracy, an excess of systems and processes created only to increase control that end up paralyzing work, an outdated command & control management style that is still ubiquitous, and of course limiting mindsets... Does this ring any bells?

In the last 16 years we have worked with CEOs and leaders of many large organizations in different parts of the world, in different industries, and in different moments of their life cycle. The majority believe that their challenges are unique to them. Our experience has shown us that the issues are more common than believed. In an effort to upgrade our services to add more value to our clients, we decided to go beyond the anecdotal stories from our clients, to find more evidence to validate Deloitte's assessment, and to find the root cause of the organizational problems, if any. In order to gain a deeper understanding of the most common organizational challenges we decided to examine the other quantitative research available.

A very interesting insight emerged when we looked at the regional results of an organizational culture survey called Cultural Transformation Tools (CTT) by Barrett Values Centre, a survey that in Asterys we tend to use for measuring the main elements of the current culture and the desired culture within companies. We realized that the main challenges are always the same, across industry, across organizational dimension, across location.

In this survey, respondents – generally all the employees, managers, and leaders of an organization, or a sample of them –

are asked to choose 10 values or behaviors that describe the current culture of the organization and 10 values or behaviors that describe the culture that they would like to experience in the future. The list of values from which respondents can choose includes both positive and potentially limiting values. Examples of the former are values such as accountability, teamwork, innovation, continuous improvement, ethics, and so on. Examples of the latter are bureaucracy, blame, internal competition, silo mentality, distrust, and many others. The share of the potentially limiting values among the total values chosen by respondents in a given company measures the organizational "entropy" or degree of dysfunction existing in the organization. We can refer to entropy also as the amount of energy that becomes dissipated rather than being used to achieve the company's goals.

A cultural entropy of 10% or lower indicates a healthy organization, as a little bit of friction can be considered natural. An entropy between 11% and 20% reflects issues requiring cultural or structural adjustment. More than that and the issues are considered "significant" (between 21% and 30% entropy), "serious" (between 31% and 40% entropy), or "critical" (over 40% entropy) and require increasing cultural and structural transformation, leadership development, and coaching – and ultimately changes in the leadership.

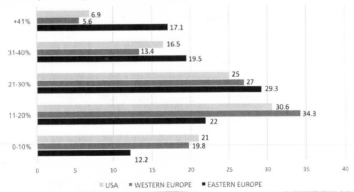

Image 1: Levels of entropy in organizations - Barrett Values Centre 2007-2016.

Looking at the overall results of organizational entropy by region (we chose to monitor North America, Western Europe, and Eastern Europe) we can notice that almost anywhere, the level of entropy is worryingly high: almost half the organizations surveyed (1,440 in these three regions) have levels of entropy above 21%, with Eastern Europe having the largest share of companies with levels above 31%.

Then our curiosity led us to examine which potentially limiting values lead to the different levels of entropy of the organizations. Not surprisingly, when looking at the top 10 values selected by respondents for level of entropy, we noticed that bureaucracy, hierarchy, control, short-term focus, silo mentality, blame, control, and information hoarding are increasingly present and influence how people work, collaborate, and achieve goals – thereby also influencing organizational performance and the ability to innovate and change.

[handwritten: Selection of top lovalues per level of entropy which organizes the org. specific data]

0-10%	11-20%	21-30%	31-40%	≥41%
teamwork	teamwork	bureaucracy	bureaucracy	bureaucracy
customer satisfaction	customer satisfaction	results orientation	cost reduction	confusion
commitment	continuous improvement	cost reduction	confusion	silo mentality
continuous improvement	results orientation	teamwork	hierarchy	cost reduction
quality	commitment	confusion	silo mentality	short-term focus
continuous learning	accountability	customer satisfaction	results orientation	hierarchy
professionalism	organizational growth	continuous improvement	short-term focus	blame
organizational growth	achievement	hierarchy	control	control
accountability	quality	accountability	long hours	long hours
humor/ fun	goals orientation	short-term focus	blame	information hoarding

[handwritten: did not include cost red.]

Image 2: Top 10 Current values in organizations by level of entropy. Source: Barrett Values Center. Data from 2,463 cultural values assessments in 77 countries, 2016.

Let's look at what those limiting values imply.

Bureaucracy can be a form of control. Too much bureaucracy can block creativity and entrepreneurial spirit, and may erode accountability and trust. Bureaucracy can lead to ineffectiveness.

Hierarchy can become potentially limiting when position dictates the quality and degree of relationships for all involved.

Power and status can become the focal points.

Information hoarding happens when managers withhold information in an effort to maintain or gain power and status. When information is not shared freely, creativity and trust are completely lost.

Confusion may reflect the lack of clarity among employees about organizational direction, priorities, and responsibilities. It slows down performance and leads to non-optimal decisions.

Control may imply a lack of trust in others. Control can block innovation, creativity, accountability, and entrepreneurship. Control may sometimes be seen as a positive value only when it concerns financial matters.

Short-term focus leads to actions aimed at a short-term advantage, and is generally motivated by the need to provide shareholders with quarter-on-quarter financial gains and not by a higher organizational purpose. Short-term focus may lead to the exploitation of resources, unethical decisions, a decrease in social engagement and a lack of long-term sustainability.

Silo mentality may be a reflection of disconnection, lack of knowledge sharing, and hindered capability for achieving common goals and community. It generally hinders innovation and generates internal conflicts.

Long hours are often a by-product of short-term focus: in an effort to optimize and make the organization more and more efficient, people are exploited and their working time is expanded to unhealthy levels. Stress levels have been constantly increasing in the last twenty years and 66% of workers in Europe attribute their stress to excessive workload. The total cost of mental health disorders related to stress in Europe (both work and non-work related) is estimated to be 240 billion Euros per year, of which 57% or 136 billion Euros indicate lost productivity, including sick leave.[1]

Blame is about focusing on finding fault for mistakes and problems instead of learning from them. In a control-driven organization the overemphasis on finger-pointing causes people to avoid accountability and risk-taking.

Thus, no matter the company you work for, its dimension, its location... you have a high probability of working in a toxic environment that leaves you unable to express your full potential.

the authors discussed the problems in high-entropy organizations were common among the regional orgs and could be boiled down to to common limiting aspects /

The paradoxes of current large hierarchy-based organizations

During the many years in which we have helped CEOs and Management Teams to develop cultures that could align with their strategies, we have found that the characteristics of the existing and unquestioned organizational structures and systems conflicted greatly with the expected desired culture.

Very recently a client asked us for an intervention in their commercial division. In consideration of all the new challenges of the client's industry and the need to develop stronger and more trusting relationships with their distributors, they aimed to increase their forecast accuracy and to respond to the issues that naturally and regularly emerged in their customer relationships in a prompt and pro-active way. The internal discussion on the ways to reach this goal led to an acknowledgement that all employees had to change their mindset and the way they work. So the commercial division's management team opted to undertake a change initiative.

At the time we were brought in, they had already identified a number of actions and changes to their processes and attitudes, and assigned each action/change to a task force for

---

1 Source: European Agency for Safety and Health at Work 2014-2015.

implementation, but after some time (well, actually, a few years…) it seemed that none of the actions had been implemented. The help they needed from us was to instigate the urge to change and to provide employees with a practical methodology to accomplish their action plans.

We asked the owner of this initiative some questions to explore the context and develop a better understanding of the reasons why the employees had failed to implement such a well-structured plan. Then we found out that it was the management team who, without any input from or involvement of the employees, had decided on the change initiative, on the actions to be implemented and even on the composition and leadership of the task forces.

It was pretty obvious to us (but not really to the client) that in a situation where there is a group of a select privileged few (the managers) who can make change decisions, and another group of the not-so privileged many (the employees) who have no say and who can only implement the top-down orders, the employees will have an instinctive reaction of resistance and passive opposition to decisions to which they could not contribute.

How can an external facilitator "instigate" the urge to implement a plan, when employees have been treated like they aren't smart enough to identify potential solutions to problems, to organize themselves in task forces, and to decide on outputs they could be counted on to deliver?

The vast majority of people interventions that the Human Resource department initiates inside large organizations collide with the ways in which the organization is structured and with the systems that regulate the work. Hierarchical structures and systems shape and reinforce ineffective behaviors in a way that most often goes unnoticed and undealt with. People interventions thus create unrealistic expectations and outcomes that even when positive are not sustainable in the long run, because employees will go back to the behaviors that structures and systems intrinsically reward.

Hierarchical structures and systems generate and reinforce the same behaviors that the organization would like to dismantle. So any change that the management team wants to implement in the organization becomes difficult, requiring an enormous amount of energy, effort, and money.

In sailing, it's like wanting to make headway by sailing directly into the wind. It is physically impossible with current sailing technology. However, if the destination is located against the wind, a sailor can still reach it by sailing at forty-five degree angles to the oncoming wind and alternating the direction of those angles. It takes much more time and effort compared to the straightforward navigation when the wind blows laterally or from the back of the sailboat.

Adopting a non-hierarchical structure means navigating with the tailwind, allowing rapid and direct progress without unnecessary obstruction.

It is no accident that most companies are organized in a hierarchical fashion. The structures and systems an organization adopts are generally designed for the efficient achievement of goals, and the hierarchical format seems the best choice when it is introduced. The problem is that these structures and systems are never scrutinized or challenged when conditions change.

To have a better understanding of how the hierarchical structure became mainstream, it is useful to go back to the beginning of the 20th century in the United States, where job-shop manufacturing was shifting to mass production. Companies needed an effective way to perform the work and a strong control of the manufacturing process.

The thinkers in that period, Frederick Taylor in the United States and Henri Fayol in France, saw the organization as a machine and developed principles and systems that suggested how to structure the company for maximum efficiency and productivity.

These principles and systems included: job classification; top-down authority structures; separation of roles between those making decisions and those implementing the decisions; reporting structures; division into functional departments; standard operating processes; and a strong focus on specialization. The vertically, hierarchically structured organization became the classic structure that after more than a century is still applied in the vast majority of large organizations.

The elements that describe a hierarchical organization are: the distinction between the role of superior (to whom the decision-making power is assigned) and the role of subordinate (who is expected to accept the authority of the superior); an extensive system of formal rules; a vertical chain of communication; and a focus on division of labor, regulation, and control.

The economic growth after World War II allowed companies that had survived the Great Depression to experience a sudden increase in size and geographic dispersion, an increasing complexity, and a need for more creativity and innovation.

The matrix structure developed as an effort to share resources among business units, to mitigate excessive specialization, and to foster cross-fertilization of ideas by having people working in project groups with experts from other functions. Even if the matrix structure solved some of the limitations of the traditional structure, it was still developed under the same hierarchical organizational mindset. Furthermore, the double reporting (employees having a functional boss and a line boss) increased complexity and potential conflicts of power.

More recently, many organizations have moved to a flatter structure, in order to reduce the hierarchical layers and allow more collaboration among teams. Notwithstanding all the reorganizations, the disadvantages of the hierarchical structure remain.

Without a doubt, the vertical structure (with a long or short chain-of-command) generates several organizational paradoxes: expectations and hopes that conflict with the obvious outcome of the underlying operating system. Let's explore some of the most common paradoxes.

Expectation of trust vs. control-driven systems

Almost all the systems in place in the average organization (KPIs, reporting, assessments, rules, policies and regulations, performance management appraisals, just to name a few) have been put in place for the purpose of controlling employees. The role of Manager has been created for this same purpose: to control employees.

The basic assumption underlying these forms of control is that employees cannot be trusted and should be closely monitored. Even if not openly stated, this is the message that people get. If a CEO or a Management Team aspires to develop more trust among their workers, they need to rethink the way the whole company can demonstrate trust in its people.

Expectation of risk-taking vs. punishment for mistakes

The CEO of a major pharmaceutical company once asked us for an intervention to inspire his employees to take on more risks. The CEO aspired to see more innovation and creativity and had identified the fear of making mistakes as the main issue hindering people's potential. When we asked how the organization dealt with mistakes, he revealed that he was keen to consider mistakes as opportunities for learning, but that he could accept only one mistake of the same kind. This seemed fair enough... make sure you always make new mistakes.

Then we interviewed a sample of employees on the same topic and we realized that the context as they perceived it was very different from the CEO's vision. Employees worked with a strong fear of consequences for their mistakes and they gave us some examples of what could happen: they mentioned that one day a director in Spain just disappeared from the company. He left, without a goodbye or explanation.

They all speculated that he was fired because he did something wrong. They mentioned a few other cases of this kind of overt or covert punishment. Middle managers and executives were not as flexible toward mistakes as the CEO thought and the HR department didn't have a policy of transparency, so that an aura of secrecy surrounded any layoff or disciplinary procedure. Employees all valued their jobs, so they learned to keep their heads down, to always be on the safe side, and to avoid taking risks.

We did set up a training program to develop trust, but without an intervention in the system itself, we knew that we wouldn't be able to achieve the best possible result, especially in the long term.

Expectation of autonomy and self-direction vs. rigid regulations

Increasing complexity and competition require organizations to respond to customer issues promptly and to develop solutions that may not have been tried before. In this context, it is imperative for organizations that employees be more autonomous, to better answer customers' needs or generally find creative solutions to emerging problems. But this expectation crashes into the zillion procedures and processes, including authorization processes, that suffocate people's initiative.

Hugh O'Byrne describes one of their sales processes that sales reps had a problem with: "When I interviewed the person who designed the process I realized that there are 120 steps to this model, including several internal authorization steps. Imagine if I have just a £1,000 sales deal… following this process makes the sale not worthwhile. We need to simplify the rules and allow people to make decisions at their level."

More autonomy can happen only if the individual is not tied by rigid, binding, time-consuming policies and regulations.

Expectation of entrepreneurial attitude vs. subordination

This is another wild dream of many top managers: inspiring an entrepreneurial spirit in employees, so that they can respond to a situation more quickly and with stronger personal ownership. Unfortunately this dream fails to become reality when subordination is in place. The characteristic of entrepreneurs is the freedom to dream and realize, to take risks because they don't need to justify or build consensus around their actions.

Once it is established that there is a boss and a subordinate, well… inevitably a reality is created in which the boss takes charge and the subordinate obeys and gives up power. It's in the nature of the boss-subordinate relationship and, as we will learn later on in the chapter, it doesn't depend on the will or competence of the individuals.

Expectation of employee engagement vs. top-down decisions

In the last decade or so, employee engagement has risen to one of the top concerns in organizations. The 2011-2012 State of the Global Workplace, an international study by the Gallup Institute on this topic, shows that only 13% of employees feel engaged. The rest of the employees are either "not engaged"

(63%) or "actively disengaged" (24%). And these numbers have not changed much in the last 15 years, despite increasing investments in employee engagement initiatives.

Of course there are many factors that contribute to the lack of engagement among employees, including a lack of trust (see previous points), perceived lack of respect toward people, or lack of transparency. But a great deal of engagement is lost when people are not included in organizational decisions and when they are not allowed to make autonomous decisions on issues that fall under their sphere of responsibility.

Expectation of collaboration vs. individual reward system

This is a classic. Any Management Team we have ever spoken to desires to see more collaboration within their teams. A lot of effort and money goes into team-building activities, alcohol-fueled Friday evenings out, and so on. But unless the focus of the reward system shifts from the individual to the group, employees will focus on the incentives that bring them personal rewards. The very idea of advancing one's career in a vertically-structured organization pushes people into competition, not collaboration.

Expectation of agility vs. bureaucracy

CEOs invest a lot of money in agility programs, hoping to simplify how people work and to speed up company processes, but because they don't fully trust people, they keep the entire control & compliance structure in place. Agility can't be achieved without getting rid of policies, procedures, authorization levels, complicated processes, norms and ultimately managers. As Hugh O'Byrne told us: "In our company, the employee manual is 40/50 pages. Nordstrom's is only one statement: 'Use you best judgment, always.' I highly admire a company that goes that far. It's as if the management said: we train you to do the right things, then we trust you and we'll give you the support mechanism that allows you to give us your best contribution."

Does a company that trusts its employees to use "their best judgment, always" need complicated and tortuous ways to control them? We don't think so.

The idea that the structure and the systems of an organization shape people's behavior is not new. Chris Argyris, Professor Emeritus at Harvard Business School and co-founder of Organization Development, known for seminal work on learning organizations, was among the first to argue that a rigid hierarchical structure paves the way for a shift in behavior from active toward passive, from self-management toward dependency, from equal to subordinate. Other researchers (R. Merton, P. M. Blau, James Worthy, to name just a few) suggest that hierarchy causes conservatism, conformity, domination of individuals, low output, low morale, and decreased innovation.

A recent study by Louisiana State University's Richard D. White, Jr. has built an argument supporting the hypothesis that a rigid hierarchy restricts an individual's moral development and ultimately adversely affects ethical behavior.

The correlation between hierarchy and moral development is reinforced by studies suggesting that hierarchical organizations have a negative effect upon small group conformity behavior, obedience to authority, and groupthink.

In a famous experiment set up by Stanley Milgram, a Yale professor and social psychologist, a person in authority orders study participants to inflict a subject with an increasing intensity of electric shock (although in reality no shock is given), ostensibly to gauge the effect of punishment on the subject's ability to memorize content. Milgram expected most participants to refuse the order but found out that 65% of the study participants obeyed the order and administered the highest level of shock. The insight for Milgram was that individuals in a hierarchy become passive players and enter a state in which autonomy, responsibility, and moral judgment are suspended. According to Milgram, *"the essence of obedience consists in the fact that a person comes to view himself as the instrument for carrying out another person's wishes, and he therefore no longer sees himself as responsible for his actions."*

Org. leadership has not recognized that hierarchy structures in outcomes contradictory to those they are looking for, & dictates culture based on common & predictable reaction from members. The paradoxes of achievement vs. control persist.

Technical and adaptive solutions

The Founding Director of the Center for Public Leadership at the John F. Kennedy School of Government at Harvard University, Professor Ronald Heifetz makes a distinction between technical and adaptive challenges. Technical challenges are those for which the competences and skills required to succeed already exist within the current paradigm or mindset, although they are not yet known to the individual person who must acquire them. To take one example, let us say you will have to face the challenge of being able to sail a vessel during a storm.

To be able to do this, you will have to study sailing and meteorology and follow the necessary theoretical and practical courses that allow you to acquire the knowledge and experience required to maneuver a ship in difficult weather conditions. All this knowledge exists already and you don't have to question yourself or the conventions of sailing in order to learn it. At the most, you may have to deal with your own apprehension.

Adaptive challenges, in contrast, require that the person develops a completely new mindset, new values, and new ways of learning. Adaptive challenges are connected to transformation, either personal or – in the case of business challenges – collective.

They require us to question the assumptions and beliefs underlying our way of seeing and interpreting ourselves, others, the circumstances, and the world, and to be able to reformulate them. The problem is that leaders in organizations often mistake adaptive for technical challenges and continue to apply technical solutions which inevitably fail or fall short of their potential.

Let's consider how corporations have tried to solve their

organizational issues. In the last 30 years we have seen a number of fancy corporate initiatives, some of which have lasted for several decades, others which emerged and disappeared in a matter of a few years: Total Quality programs, the matrix structure, Six Sigma interventions, Lean initiatives, leadership development programs, flatter organizations, and more recently Smart Working.

The results of these initiatives generally fall far short of reaching their full potential and after a few years the company is ready to move on to its next transformation effort. The reason is that all these initiatives are implemented within the same mindset that created the problems in the first place. They are technical solutions to adaptive challenges.

In biology the term "adaptive pressure" defines a situation in which the effective response to the surrounding environment is not included in the possibilities and current capabilities of the organism. This means that the organism must observe its processes and "discern" what still works and what needs to be abandoned, and this requires a transformation, if the organism is to survive successfully in an environment that has changed. The same process should be undertaken by a person, company, or organization when the contextual conditions change or when the old strategies are no longer effective.

In the last decade, it has become increasingly obvious that we are under "adaptive pressure": the solutions to the most common corporate issues are not to be found in the current capability of the organization. *Organizations under "adaptive" pressure have to establish what's no longer working & develop new organizational capacities / solutions to new problems in order to adapt / transform.*

It's the system, baby!

When a problem emerges in an organization, the classical response of the managers and top executives is to focus on the symptom of the problem and to identify the most effective solution to that particular symptom.

"We had people leaving accusing us of being too bureaucratic,"

shares Hugh O'Byrne, former VP Global Sales Center Excellence, Digital Business Group at IBM Europe: *"We had to try to improve productivity. I hired a Six Sigma consultant. Among his findings, there was one that hit me: there were 57 steps in a particular process. Way too many steps. I went to the head of the unit and shared the data from the consultant. He gave me his ok to move forward and change."*

"In my former company I heard constant complaints from Hong Kong toward the US team, and vice versa. Or Hong Kong against Bali," Miles Graham, former Chief Operation Officer at John Hardy remembers. *"We had 200 cross-geography touch points, decisions made cross-geographically. These people's complaints were a red flag on our processes. So I restructured the business to move from 200 to 17 touch points only."*

"When I encountered organizational issues," recalls Laura Donnini, former CEO of the Italian publishing company RCS, now CEO of HarperCollins Italia, *"I looked at either change management initiatives, by evaluating the company climate and setting up off-site retreats to re-align my leadership team around our values and strategy, or organizational re-designs, with or without external consultants."*

These approaches are all valid and certainly generate some positive results. But they are driven by a mechanistic approach to problem-solving: they focus on the single broken or badly-functioning part of the organization, without considering the interrelations and dynamics between the various parts and without addressing the underlying cause of the problem. So a solution is adopted that puts a patch on the symptom but ignores the consequences that the solution then causes in other parts of the company.

One of the most typical consequences of ignoring the inner dynamics and interrelations in a system is the resistance to change. Donato Iacovone, EY Managing Partner Italy, Spain, and

Portugal worries that *"The biggest risk is to resist change. This is lethal because customers are changing dramatically, and so are their needs. Either we anticipate change – at least travelling at the same speed – or we will be kicked out of the market."*

"Once I got the agreement from the head of the unit to simplify the unnecessarily complex process," Hugh O'Byrne admits, *"then the Six Sigma expert reduced the steps from 57 to 10. Months of work went into this but then employees found it difficult to change. Resistance happened mostly at the level of first and second line managers. I feel frustration and then anger about how difficult it is to get people to change."*

Other times, the solution implemented has a positive impact in the short term, but then the problem re-emerges in other forms or in other parts of the company.

The discipline that helps us consider the organization as a network of interdependent parts is System Thinking.

System Thinking is a management discipline that focuses on the linkages and dynamics among the different parts of an organization, considered as a "living system". This "system" includes several entities (for example structure, policies, practices, and people) that may be subdivided into other sub-systems. All these components are interdependent and work together to try to accomplish a common aim (Deming, 1986).

System Thinking suggests that we need to learn how the whole affects the parts and how the parts affect the whole if we want to solve problems arising in the system. This approach is revolutionizing many fields of study, since in the Western world we have been used to seeing problems from a mechanistic point of view, meaning that the parts are independent from the whole.

We can see this clearly in traditional Western medicine. If we go to the doctor with a health issue, say, a stomach pain, the doctor will most likely focus on alleviating or curing the symptoms, not addressing the underlying causes of the problem – which may well recur.

Systems can be closed, if they are relatively independent of their environment, or open, if they constantly exchange energy, information, and material with their environment. Business organizations are highly open systems, as they exchange products, services, value, and information with their environment.

If we consider the organization as a living system, then the way we look at problems and opportunities needs to shift from the traditional reductionist paradigm to the emergent systemic paradigm. This entails a shift in the paradigms underlying how we see and manage a company.

The most common paradigms related to the reductionist approach are as follows:

Managing from the parts. As we pointed out earlier, this is the belief that the organization is merely the sum of all its parts and when something breaks, it should be repaired or replaced.

Keeping the boundaries. The reductionist's approach suggests that there must be boundaries between the organization and its environment and also within the organization itself. Departments do not communicate with each other, information is used to maintain power, and there is secrecy around important corporate issues.

Linear causality provides the explanation. Everything can be explained through a linear chain of cause and effect where one event causes another event in a way that can be predictable. So managers assume that for every issue, a single cause can be isolated and dealt with. There's a lot of energy and effort dedicated to finding the reason for what occurs in order to prevent it from happening again.

Complexity is manageable. Although we all admit that organizations today have reached a certain level of complexity, many still assume that at some point, you can understand and deal with it. The belief is that it is possible to get the big picture by devoting time and effort to breaking down and analyzing the individual different parts of the company and then putting them back together.

how else do you do it?

A pivot point controls everything. There is a belief that whoever sits at the top of the organization, generally the CEO or the Managing Director, can control the direction and the speed of the organization.

Given these reductionist paradigms, people in the organization act accordingly: they expect and engage in incremental change; they protect their territories; they are part of the causality; and they control (or at least try to) people's behaviors.

System Thinking is based on a completely different set of paradigms. *axioms*

Managing from the whole. As organizations are a complex web of people, processes, and dynamics, we need to "zoom out" in order to observe and understand them. We need to move from the "dance floor" to "the balcony", as in the metaphor used by Harvard University's John F. Kennedy School of Government Professor Ronald Heifetz: "The only way you can gain both a clearer view of reality and some perspective on the bigger picture is by distancing yourself from the fray, while if you want to affect what is happening, you must return to the dance floor."

Loosening the boundaries. Network links and the diverse competencies needed for problem-solving and innovation make it impossible to define and maintain clear boundaries in an organization. The same happens outside, in the organizational environment: the evolution of markets, industries and nations creates interdependency and connections.

Non-linear causality influences events. Events can be understood only by considering that cause and effect can flow in a bidirectional fashion between two or more elements of a system instead of as a linear chain of events. Multiple causes can interact among themselves and create a possibility for more outcomes, muddying the relationship between cause and effect and confounding those wanting to understand a problem. We all believe that people's behavior in organizations should be predictable and rational, but that's not the case. We can see patterns that may indicate the probability of a future event, but we cannot predict what is going to happen.

Complexity is complex. When you approach a problem, the variables and unknowns to consider add up exponentially. While a reductionist mindset is keen to believe that at some point we can collect all the information and knowledge to solve a problem, the system thinker believes that we had better become comfortable with ambiguity and uncertainty and that we have to make decisions despite the inevitably missing information.

Control is an illusion. Managers are given authority and power over employees in order to ensure that appropriate levels of control are maintained, but control over people is an illusion. Just as the intricate web of the internet cannot be controlled, neither can organizations. Networks do not accept force, they resist it, as often happens in change programs. The only way to act upon a system is to try to influence it.

Reductionist paradigms	Systemic paradigms
Managing from the parts	Managing from the whole
Keeping the boundaries	Loosening the boundaries
Linear causality explains	Non-linear causality influences
Complexity is manageable	Complexity is complex
A pivot point controls everything	Control is an illusion

A systemic approach is essential for those who wish to understand and influence complex organizations in rapidly changing environments.

Authors are applying systems thinking to organization dynamics & management & company system approach to mechanistic approach.

It requires a paradigm shift.

Zooming out: the systemic patterns of hierarchy

As if what we just shared was not enough, we want to mention the work of Barry Oshry, a pioneer in systems thinking and former Chairman of the Department of Human Relations at Boston University. Barry and his associates have conducted experiential exercises of one to seven days in length at hundreds of organizations in the US and around the world. During all these exercises, Oshry made a simple observation. In every organization, no matter its size, industry or location, the same limiting patterns of behavior emerged. And even if a solution were implemented to improve the results, the same issues kept coming back.

What he noticed was that the problems were not being generated by the individuals, but they were systemic – meaning, shaped by the different contexts within which people operate and work relative to one another. In every organization, there are predictable dynamics that emerge from the mere fact that employees are subject to certain "conditions" typical of a hierarchical structure. And employees are blind to these dynamics. Let's explore Oshry's insights a bit more.

When we are in a relationship with an organization, we can step into one of the following spaces:

A "Top": a person who is responsible for the whole organization, or part of it, or a whole project, but needs to rely on others to achieve his/her goals;

A "Bottom": an employee who does the work but doesn't have responsibility for the whole organization, or any part of it;

A "Middle": a manager who is supposed to coordinate the work of the bottoms, meet customers' needs, and ensure the desired results for the Top;

A "Customer": someone who needs products or services from a company or a person, but who doesn't feel involved in the delivery.

When we are in one of these spaces, we enter into a

"condition" that is not necessarily related with our official role in the organizational chart but to the position we hold in each specific relationship. This condition causes us to see the world in a particular way and to respond to events and circumstances with predictable patterns of reactions. *Social psychologist*

Top, Middle, Bottom, and Customer are conditions all of us experience regardless of our hierarchical position: in any relationship, we may adopt any of the psychological conditions of the list above. In certain interactions, we are Top when we have specific responsibility for a project or a task, a whole department, or company. In other interactions, we are Bottom when we carry out a task and we face problems with our condition and/or with the condition of the system, and we think higher-ups ought to be taking care of those problems but are not. In other interactions we are Middle when we are experiencing conflicting demands, priorities, and pressures coming at us from two or more individuals or groups. And in other relationships, we are a Customer, when we expect a product or service from a person or a team, to satisfy our needs.

We can experience shifts between the conditions of Top/Middle/Bottom/Customer in any relationship. For example we are Tops when we are given the responsibility of coordinating the launch of a new product. We are Bottoms when we need to perform control on the resources we need to achieve our goals. Even a CEO is a Bottom when he/she needs a budget approval from the Regional VP. We are Middle when we find ourselves between two stakeholders with conflicting needs (i.e. being the account executive of an advertising company, "selling" the work of the creatives to a client). We are Customers when we expect from the sales marketing department the tools we need as a sales representative to promote the company products at their best.

In each of these conditions (Top/Middle/Bottom/Customer) there are unique and predictable limiting patterns which arise when we experience problems in the organization.

As Tops, when we experience problems we tend – maybe not

mistaken orange –
is more yellow

every time, but with a certain regularity – to take responsibility upon ourselves and away from others. It is like a unconscious reflex: we are the one responsible for solving the problem. We start micromanaging, we disempower others by diminishing their potential contribution, and we are so involved in everything that we lose sight of the big picture. This automatic response may be reinforced by other factors, such as the fear of appearing weak or not in charge, or our concern that delegating to others might lead to negative results for which we would still be held responsible. In any case, the pattern is always the same: taking on too much responsibility. The predictable consequence is an overload at the Top, a feeling of being overwhelmed by the continuous, difficult issues coming at us.

As Bottoms, when a problem occurs, we tend – maybe not every time, but with a certain regularity – to hold the Tops responsible for the issues, not us. It's their fault, not ours. Again, we enact this pattern unconsciously. There could be other reinforcers, such as our fear of failure, which keeps us from fixing the problem ourselves, or our loyalty to our peers, who are so adamant on blaming the Tops, or the higher-ups' attitude of keeping the Bottoms out of the problem-solving process. In any case, the pattern is always the same: blaming the Tops, with the consequence of feeling disregarded and vulnerable.

As Middles, when a problem emerges, we tend – maybe not every time, but with a certain regularity – to have a stronger connection to one stakeholder and a reduced connectivity with the other one. For example, we could connect more deeply with our direct reports in an attempt to protect them, but in so doing lose our connection with our superiors, or vice versa. When we strengthen the connection to one stakeholder to the detriment of the other one we reduce our contribution and create more complexity, producing a lack of coordination. The pattern becomes torn and the consequence is the "Middle crunch".

When we are Customers, we shift responsibility for the delivery of the product or service that we want entirely to the deliverer. We are in no way responsible, we are entitled to blame the deliverer, and we expect improvement only on their side. As a consequence we feel neglected and cheated.

All these patterns, as we mentioned, are produced by the system, not by each individual. And they are inescapable; they are dynamics that characterize any relationship under a hierarchy-based structure. It appears evident that when these dynamics occur, no training or coaching will solve the issue in the long term. The dynamics will come back again and again until:

- the people involved become aware of the system dynamics and there is a conscious effort to recognize the pattern and choose a different response; or
- there is a fundamental shift in the structure of the organization, where the conditions of Top, Bottom, Middle, and Customer are replaced by a condition of partnership in all relationships.

When we recognized these insights after a workshop where we experienced being a Top, Middle, Bottom, and Customer, a whole new horizon appeared in front of us. We realized that as consultants, coaches, and facilitators we had two choices for setting up a successful change program:

- We could do the best we can in the current paradigm, aiming at incremental change, providing our clients with effective transformational journeys that expand their employees' awareness of the system and support them in mitigating its limits, keeping the hierarchical structure in place; or
- We could embark on a journey to design a whole new "operating system" and new processes that transcend the limits of the hierarchical structure and generate a more sustainable, creative, collaborative environment.

In the last two decades we have worked with big corporations in supporting mindset and behavior transformations within the current hierarchical paradigm and we know that many companies are not ready (and some do not even need) to go that far into abandoning the hierarchical structure. Hence, we made a conscious decision to keep supporting such organizations in maximizing their leadership development effort and their change initiatives while raising their level of systemic awareness and their ability to optimize their outcomes notwithstanding their hierarchical power structure. At the same time we started to reflect on how we could advocate and inspire a new paradigm for those companies who dare to revolutionize the way they work and unleash creativity and deep fulfillment from their people. *a simply psychological schema of who is responsible / how we problem solve in positions in the heirarchy (top, middle, bottom, customer).*

The emerging future

Some companies can do well w/ leadership dev. considering this info. others are ready to revolution-ize

Before we dove into the design of a new organizational structure, we wanted to make sure we understood the emerging needs and aspirations of people in organizations.

We came back to the Cultural Transformation Tools (CTT) Regional analysis but this time we looked at the values that employees would like to see enacted in their organizations, the "desired culture".

We looked at the results by level of entropy of the organization and we had a huge surprise (well, after all that we have written thus far, it shouldn't be a surprise for you): no matter the level of entropy in the organization… all employees want the same things.

0-10%	11-20%	21-30%	31-40%	≥41%
teamwork	teamwork	accountability	accountability	accountability
continuous improvement	continuous improvement	continuous improvement	teamwork	continuous improvement
customer satisfaction	accountability	teamwork	continuous improvement	teamwork
commitment	customer satisfaction	open communication	open communication	open communication
accountability	open communication	customer satisfaction	employee recognition	information sharing
open communication	employee recognition	employee recognition	information sharing	trust
continuous learning	innovation	information sharing	trust	customer satisfaction
innovation	commitment	commitment	efficiency	leadership development
quality	quality	innovation	customer satisfaction	commitment
trust	efficiency	balance (home/work)	adaptability	coaching/mentoring
				employee recognition
				innovation

Image 3: Top 10 Desired Values in organizations by level of entropy. Source: Barrett Values Centre. Data from 2,463 cultural values assessments in 77 countries, 2016.

This data revealed to us just how pervasive certain desires are: the desire for more collaboration, more accountability, an approach to continuous improvement, more communication in the company, and a double focus on employee recognition on the one hand and customer satisfaction on the other. But it didn't give us enough insights into what changes in the organization employees think would be necessary for creating the best organization of the future.

We reviewed the main aspirations and hopes for the future which emerged from the deep structured interviews we had with CEOs and top executives. They seem to have pretty clear ideas on the future destination of companies. Many spoke about structuring the organizations in clusters or creating self-organizing teams.

Søren Hagh, Managing Director Italy, Heineken shares: "*I see self-organizing teams work quite well; I worked for Lego a few years and they are organized exactly like this. Self-organizing teams are extremely successful and I think there is an enormous amount of merit in the idea. It's an environment that demands a certain culture, where people are comfortable taking ownership for their own work, and it's going to be increasingly relevant; but also what I've witnessed is that self-organizing teams are culturally easier to implement in low-power cultures (like in Northern Europe) than in more traditionally hierarchical cultures, like Italy. But it makes people happy and satisfied and makes them efficient in their job. The direction is a very healthy one.*"

Emmanuel Mottrie, CEO TMC International: "*You need to cut the organizations into different cells, where people can take over the process. But I think a lot of people will have difficulty in changing, you need to change behaviors; the first one to do it is the CEO. He must forget his role and be on the floor again. You also must skip all unnecessary processes, get rid of the Mexican Army Syndrome (too many hierarchical levels and titles), and put the middle management back in operational roles.* You should also fight against 'meetingitis' and 'presentationitis', two serious diseases for healthy organizations."

Purpose seems a very important part of creating the right culture, engaging employees, and facilitating decision-making.

Magda Mook, CEO/Executive Director at ICF: "*It is not just that the organization must have a purpose, but it's also important what that purpose is, and if it contributes to societal progress. I think this is the shift and the paradox that we'll be observing in the next several years: more and more of even big corporations start having that social progress aspect of their work, and there is a way to having their business and doing good.*"

Georg Schroeckenfuchs, Country President and CPO Head Italy at Novartis pushes us even further: "*The key is to have a high purpose so that all employees deeply understand what the company stands for and the purpose is owned by every individual. Then we need the simplification of processes that liberates a fast decision-making process and reduces company politics. And if I can dream, I can always dream of the self-organizing teams. Does a company need teams? For sure... but does a company really need leaders? If you are able to engage employees to a level where they understand the purpose and the diverse customer needs... then do you need leaders?*"

In these interviews we had the perception that many leaders – although in some ways still unable to imagine a future, successful organization without "leaders" – are becoming ready to really embrace a revolution in their organizations and that the shift of power from leaders and supervisors to individuals and teams is the key to it. But what about the employees? Will they be ready to move in this direction?

We set up a quantitative survey to test some hypotheses relative to specific characteristics of the "organization of the future". We partnered with ResearchNow, a research company that provided us with a validated sample of 800 people working in large organizations (from 1,000 employees to 50,000 and more) – individual contributors, people managers, and top executives in various industries in the US and Europe.

The picture that the survey revealed is that employees of all levels (but more specifically the generation between 25-34 years old) are starting to demand an environment where collaboration is widespread, not just within teams but among different teams in the organization.

They want to see a company formed by a network of teams collaborating (52% of respondents), with almost one quarter of them desiring "a network of coordinated self-organizing teams, operating through shared principles, where all team members are accountable toward the whole team, with no supervisors or bosses."

How will a successful company operate 10 years from now?	%
It will operate like a hierarchical pyramid, but it will be a flatter pyramid, with just one or two layers of supervisors who manage and control the levels below and with cross-functional teams (teams that include people taking care of staff functions like HR, Administration, Legal, etc.).	28
It will operate like a hierarchical pyramid, with several layers of supervisors that manage and control the levels below and some staff functions (HR, administration, legal, public affairs, etc.) that serve all the functions.	20
Organization will be based on networked teams, and people have a number of specific projects and tasks that they undertake for their immediate supervisor/manager.	28
It will look like a network of coordinated self-organizing teams, operating through shared principles, where all team members are accountable toward the whole team, with no supervisors or bosses.	24

59% of respondents imagine an organization where decisions are decentralized and made at the team level.

How will decisions be made in the highly successful company of the future?	%
The decisions will be decentralized and made at the individual level. It is individuals who make decisions and are ultimately responsible for them, although they may ask their peers for advice.	15
The decisions will be decentralized and made at the team level. Decisions are based on consensus: in short, the team arrives at a shared agreement (it can be unanimous or by majority vote) so that everyone is heard.	32
The decisions will be decentralized and made at the team level. Decisions are based on consent, which means that the decision is validated if there are "no objections" by team members. Consent means that the team can "live with" the decision even if they don't fully agree with it.	27
The decisions will be made mainly at the higher levels of the pyramid and any decision can be invalidated by hierarchical superiors.	26

Almost half of this group would like to see "consent decision-making", which means that the decision is validated if there are "no objections" by team members. Consent means that the team can "live with" the decision even if they don't fully agree with it. We will come back to this topic later in Chapter Four.

When considering the source of the decisions, less than half the respondents believe that decisions will be determined by the management's orientation or by the direct manager considering the company policies.

41% of respondents believe that decisions will stem from a shared set of guiding principles and values and 14% believe that decisions will stem from people's best judgment.

What will be the source of the decisions?	%
Decisions will be determined by the direct manager, considering the constellation of established policies and rules.	22
Decisions will be determined by the orientation and priorities of senior management.	23
Decisions will stem from a shared set of guiding principles and values.	41
Decisions will stem from people's best judgment	14

The expectation about transparency of information is notable. 39% expect that most of the information should be widely available, with the exception of sensitive data (financials and compensation and what is restricted by law), with 25% expecting all information to be available in real time to all, including company financials and compensation, except what is restricted by law. These two groups make up 64% of the sample wanting a very transparent organization. Only 13% of respondents imagine that in the future, information should be released on a need-to-know basis by the direct manager or the management, and the profile of this group is predominantly top executives in very large organizations with over 50,000 employees. We can guess why some leaders want to keep their hands on information instead of making it available to the entire workforce.

How is information shared in the highly successful company of the future?	%
Information is released on a need-to-know basis by the immediate manager or the management	13
Information is easily accessible and held by the various departments or units that produce it. Some specific information is available only to top management.	23
Most of the information is widely available, with the exception of sensitive data (financials and compensation and what is restricted by law)	39
All information is available in real time to all, including company financials and compensations, except what is restricted by law.	25

The expectation of different degrees of a "smart working" option is shared by 77% of respondents, of which 41% imagine the office as "the primary place for many, while others enjoy a flexible location (home or other locations) so that the office becomes for them a place where you go to meet colleagues and work collaboratively on specific projects"; and 36% imagine that the office "is the hub for the few occasions when employees need to collaborate in person".

How will the workplace look 10 years from now?	%
The office is the hub for the few occasions when employees need to collaborate in person. People work when and where it is most appropriate for them, their colleagues, and their function, working in different places and settings to suit their tasks and mood.	36
The office is the primary place for many, while others enjoy a flexible location (home or other locations) so that the office becomes for them a place where you go to meet colleagues and work collaboratively on specific projects	41
The office is the primary place of work for everyone, with a regular "office time" during which employees must show up, focus on their individual tasks, and work at fixed desks.	23

Men and women here have a slightly different perspective, with the latter group showing more interest in flexibility. The two options related to smart working are chosen respectively by 46% and 35% of women and 36% and 37% of men.

We also tested different options in terms of types of collaboration, degree of managerial control over teams, degree of top-down direction, presence of systems and processes, performance management, and remuneration. The outcome of the survey presented us with interesting insights on how employees, managers, and top executives imagine the organization of the future and it gave us a clear idea of the direction to follow with our project.

There is tremendous support among the workforce for work being organized by a network of teams 37-, where decisions are decentralized at the team level, stem from a guiding set of principles, in a transparent organiz., w/ flexibility for work w/ the office being collaborative space.

Self-governance delivers

A groundbreaking study developed by LRN and independently conducted by the Boston Research Group, in collaboration with Research Data Technology and The Center for Effective Organizations at the University of Southern California, provides very useful insights related to how governance, culture, and leadership influence behavior and impact performance. In the HOW Report[2] the observations by 36,000-plus employees in 18 countries, from the C-Suite to the junior ranks, were analyzed and classified.

The study results suggest that all companies fit into one of three archetypal categories. The first archetype is called "blind obedience," and it depicts the typical "command-and-control" leadership in an organization characterized by formal authority and strict control mechanisms. The second archetype is represented by the "informed acquiescence" organizations, where systems and processes regulate all aspects of the business, and where performance is measured and rewarded, or the lack of it punished. Both "blind obedience" and "informed acquiescence" are characterized by the classical hierarchical shape and authority. The third archetype is based on "self-governance," where people are trusted to do their best for the advancement of their companies and where they tend to collaborate and innovate. In this archetype the company has developed a shared purpose and common values.

Funnily enough, the three archetypes reflect the evolution of the organizational design in the last 150 years.

The most relevant insight from the study is that companies truly built on purpose, guided by values, and permeated with trust (the "self-governance" archetype) experience significant advantages over the competition. They scored the highest on every one of the 14 performance outcomes evaluated by the study:

---

2 For the whole report: http://howmetrics.lrn.com/.

- 93% of employees at high-trust and truly values-based businesses observe financial performance greater than their competitors vs. 48% of those at strict top-down organizations.

- Employees functioning in a high trust organization are 22 times more likely to take a beneficial risk – which, in turn, enables eight times the level of innovation as compared to the competition.

- When it comes to loyalty, 92% of employees of businesses based on values and trust plan to be working for their company in a year, compared to 46% of those in strict top-down organizations. 98% would recommend their values and trust-based company to a friend vs. just 33% at strict top-down organizations.

- 99% of high-trust and values-based companies observe highly satisfied customers vs. 42% of top-down organizations.

- Employees at high-trust, values-inspired companies are 92% more likely to observe high levels of innovation relative to the competition.

- Further, in high-trust, values-inspired companies, only 24% of employees observed misconduct or unethical behaviors, compared to 47% in low-trust, non-values focused organizations.

The study also highlights the fact that only 1 in 30 companies meet the standard of being based on values and trust. Just 11% of organizations foster high-values environments where employees are encouraged to take risks, make decisions, and innovate around products, services, and processes. Only 1 in 5 respondents strongly agree there is a high level of trust in their company.

Although these self-governing companies are still rare (at least for now), they experience the highest levels of resilience, employee loyalty, customer satisfaction, and financial performance. Companies that excel at "doing good" are those whose decision-making throughout the company is animated by the highest levels of trust and values-driven cultures – with business outcomes that give them profound advantages in the marketplace. There are 3 archetypes of orgs., from a study they show that high trust, value centered orgs w/ collaboration perform higher

Our approach to the very simple task of creating a revolution

When considering the processes and tools that we would need to use to attempt to create a new organizational design that would overcome the limits of the hierarchical structure, we had no doubt. We would use a Design Thinking approach. What we liked about Design Thinking was its human-centered approach to problem-solving and innovation, which combines people's needs and aspirations with what technology makes possible and what is economically viable.

As we shared before, we started with a set of deep structured interviews with 20 CEOs and Executives of large multinational organization branches in different countries, from Canada to Germany, from Hong Kong to France, from the US to Italy. These interviews were aimed at developing a better understanding of the current organizational challenges as seen from a top manager's point of view; understanding the emotions involved in discovering and addressing the challenges; the rationales for the decisions Executives take; the deeper aspirations and desires they held for their companies; the perceived limits related to their organization's current structure, culture, systems and processes, and leadership; and finally what they dream of for the future.

These interviews helped us in shaping a persona, meaning a reliable and realistic representation of our key potential customer, and the customer's journey through organizational pitfalls.

In parallel with the interviews we conducted extensive research to collect information and knowledge about alternative structures to hierarchy, such as open organizations, self-managing teams, Sociocracy, Holacracy, peer-based accountability systems, and the like. With a deeper understanding of all these elements we started to conceive and prepare an overall draft idea of the solution.

We then set up the quantitative research questionnaire and submitted it to 800 employees, managers, and top executives in the US and Europe. We have shared the main results in the previous pages.

Subsequently, the Design Thinking task force brainstormed ideas to move past obvious solutions and into breakthrough insights. We came up with a draft of the "AEquacy" idea and the framework that united structure, culture, systems, and people for a feasible, sustainable, and scalable proposal.

At that point, we needed to understand how our customers – decision-makers with the power to initiate a shift toward a new organizational concept in their organization – would understand, interact with, and react to our idea. We created a prototype of the structure and we tested it with a group of CEOs and HR Executives.

We created a simple, physical representation of the AEquacy structure, which was presented to our group of testers in order to observe, record, judge, and measure the customer's general behavior, interactions, and reactions to the overall design. These earlier versions are known in Design Thinking as prototypes. The test went unexpectedly well, with some useful suggestions and input and without any of the pushback which, to be honest, we had been expecting.

This prototyping-testing phase was incredibly useful for us. We strongly believe that the development of aequal principles and solutions will never be definitive. The process will be iterative, with cycles of prototyping and testing, and every implementation will offer the possibility of incorporating our customers' experience and ideas into an ever-evolving organizational design.

they conducted research deep into executive thinking, alternative structures, & presented a prototype to gauge responsiveness,

Viewpoints inspiring our work

There are a few ideas or viewpoints that guided our exploration of an operating system that could replace hierarchy and overcome its pitfalls. Some of these are ideas or viewpoints that have always influenced our thinking and the way we design and deliver our programs. Some of them emerged as ideas that felt right, that honor being human and support our individual striving to learn and contribute.

- The organization as a living system

As we have already shared, the idea of the "organization as a machine" has dominated the business world since industrialization. We do not dispute that this clear division of the company into sub-units – with authority assigned according to hierarchy, the conformity of each sub-unit to rules and regulations, and the specialization of employees – provided business owners with a manageable way to expand and internationalize their companies and that it produced results until the post-World War II period. But the limits of this worldview have been experienced everywhere and not only make the organizations unsustainable, but they leave people feeling disengaged and frustrated.

We need to replace old, rigid organizational paradigms and to experiment with new viewpoints that allow us to be effective in a context of rapidly increasing change and complexity, while simultaneously allowing us to build a sense of meaning in our lives.

We believe that the idea of the organization as a living system is the antidote to the ineffective view of the organization as a machine. By definition, living systems are open, self-organizing systems that are able to interact with their environment and exchange matter and energy. And furthermore, living systems are... alive! Living systems are resilient, adaptive, and creative because they enact an open and free-flowing pattern of relationships.[3]

They have a self-integrating property. "This means that by itself, the living system integrates divergent contributions into a convergent whole in a dynamic relationship internally and externally, in an ongoing process of self-organization and self-creation. In other words, it's what makes the living system alive."[4]

- Conscious business

In 2010, a group of enlightened CEOs and consultants gave birth to a movement called Conscious Capitalism. Conscious Capitalism stems from the theory of corporate social responsibility and it is an approach to business that better reflects the current state of the world, our responsibilities as human beings and business leaders, and the potential of businesses to make a positive impact in the world. Conscious organizations do not reject the pursuit of profit, but emphasize doing so in a manner that integrates the interests of all major stakeholders. Such organizations are inspired and guided by a higher purpose that considers and expresses the interests of all the stakeholders, helping to make visible all the interdependencies across them. They aspire to create economic, emotional, spiritual, intellectual, and ecological wealth for all involved, from employees to customers to suppliers and other relevant stakeholders. They are led by leaders who feel accountable to serve the company purpose, the people who interact with their organization, and the planet. These leaders continuously develop self-awareness and system awareness; they are humble, compassionate, and willing to approach all their relationships with a win-win mentality.

---

3 The new principles of organizations as living systems are based on the works of chemists Ilya Prigogine and Manfred Eigen; biologists Conrad Waddington and Paul Weiss; anthropologist Gregory Bateson, systems theorists Erich Jantsch and Ervin Laszlo; and physicist Fritjof Capra.

4 Michelle Holliday of Cambium Consulting.

- Equality[5]

We believe that unless we abolish hierarchy, we cannot develop creative, collaborative relationships. We believe that we need to avoid any form of subordination if we want to create an environment where people can self-organize, self-direct themselves, and unleash their full potential. We have explored recent self-managing based structures such as Sociocracy and Holacracy. We consider both of them very good attempts at creating a new and more sustainable approach to organization, and we were inspired by some of their ideas. However, in both systems some forms of subordination remain. In Holacracy, for example, a particular member of a "Circle" (the term Holacracy uses for "team"), called the Lead Link, defines priorities and strategies for the Circle instead of giving the team the possibility to discuss and determine team priorities and strategies as a group. Research[6] has shown that one of the foundations of intrinsic motivation is autonomy in making decisions that impact an individual's work. In our opinion, having one person making decisions about strategies (the "how we reach our goals") of a whole group is disrespectful toward all group members and demotivating.

Even certain terminology in Holacracy maintains some form of subordination. When a Circle decides to expand its activities by creating a new circle, the original Circle becomes a "Super-Circle" and the newborn structure is called a "Sub-Circle", suggesting that one Circle is superior and the other is inferior.

Sociocracy proposes a structure formed by a hierarchy of circles, so that even if each circle is given authority to manage itself, there is still a hierarchical system of coordination and control.

---

5 Interestingly, in a web search for hierarchy antonyms, we found that 110 out of 111 antonyms presented mean "chaos, disorder, disorganization". What does this say about our mindset towards hierarchy?
6 *Drive: The Surprising Truth About What Motivates Us* by Daniel Pink, 2009.

In our reflections, we realize that true partnership and full accountability can happen only when any form of subordination is abandoned and members of the organizations are trusted to be capable of self-direction, not just self-management.

- Transparency

People have become accustomed to the possibility of accessing any information in real time thanks to the internet. The younger generation, in particular, is so exposed to information that they don't expect it to be filtered. The demand for accessibility of information has now expanded to the workplace. We are not just talking about the information customers want to access regarding a company, its products, its practices, and its values. The list of Desired Values in Image 3 earlier in this Chapter shows that "open communication" is one of the top values/behaviors that employees desire to see in their organizations.

When a company keeps information and decisions secret, this creates distrust among its employees. The decisions are perceived as arbitrary and based on management preferences, and when this happens, there is a sense of inequality and unfairness.

To fill in the information gap, people indulge in rumors and speculations that take energy away from the work that really matters. Information hoarding is also used by individual managers or groups to maintain or strengthen their power and authority. The consequence is that problem solving and innovation become unnecessarily complicated.

When information and knowledge are openly shared, employees are encouraged to contribute to the process of delivering decisions and solutions. This allows people to see the linkages and interdependencies among the different teams, and to gain a better understanding of how they contribute to the success of the organization, because anyone can see what all other teams are doing. Decisions are also wiser and more inclusive of the input of relevant stakeholders, because they can be monitored by anyone who is affected by them.

In our research on what was already available for companies wanting to move toward a new, decentralized organization, we found many examples of interesting practices by both non-profit and for-profit consulting companies, namely Sociocracy and Holacracy; by pioneering companies testing distributed authority, such as Gore in the United States or TMC in Europe; and by the existing literature on Open Organizations and Peer-based Organizations.

Whenever we found that a practice was effective and could be useful to our project, we decided to include it in our framework, without trying to reinvent the wheel.

Introducing AEquacy

AEquacy is a leaderless organizational design and operating system that changes the paradigm of the traditional, hierarchical organization and paves the way for greater innovation, collaboration, and performance. We can imagine AEquacy as an organizational "kernel",[7] a new, revolutionary operating system that overcomes the limits of the hierarchical organization and expands individual, team, and organizational potential. AEquacy can be displayed as a radial, equalitarian structure of self-organizing, peer-coordinated teams, in which people are considered associates instead of employees and serve the organizational purpose autonomously.

We chose the name AEquacy (from the Latin aequum: equality, fairness) to emphasize the absence of hierarchy and the equal right of all members of the organization to participate in decision-

---

7 The kernel is a computer program that is the core of a computer's operating system, with complete control over everything in the system. It is the first program loaded on start-up.

making. A company which adopts AEquacy is thus an aequal organization.

In aequal organizations people can perform at their best because they have total control over their work, clarity about the organizational direction and access to all information to make the best decisions.

AEquacy is based on a framework that determines the main elements in four areas that need to be in place for a successful implementation of (or transition to) this new operating system.

We will expand these areas and elements in the next four chapters, but wish to provide the overall idea here.

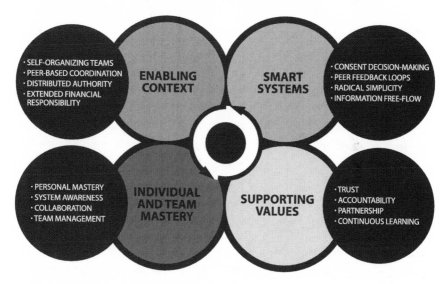

Image 4: The AEquacy framework of operating principles

In our experience supporting large organizations in implementing change programs, we learned that there are four main areas that need to be considered and aligned if the change is to stick:

1) A **context** that provides the conditions for the new organization to develop. It's like making sure that a plant has sufficient exposure to sun, water, and nutrients to grow.

In AEquacy the main elements of an enabling context are:

a. A structure of self-organizing teams that work in full autonomy, advancing the purpose of the company;

b. A system of peer-based coordination that maintains alignment without reverting to rank-based control;

Structural axioms

c. Distributed authority, to make sure that decision-making happens where the issues emerge, in any part of the organization;

d. Extended financial responsibility, by assigning each team a Profit & Loss account they are responsible for.

2) Development of a few essential **values** whose embedding is the sine qua non for AEquacy to run effectively. These values are:

a. **Trust**: when there is no formal controlling function, people need to develop their own trustworthiness and trust in one another;

b. **Accountability**: in the absence of bosses, people should consider themselves accountable toward one another and their organization and be able to report, and be responsible for, the resulting consequences of their actions;

c. **Partnership** is the quality of equal relationships, when we move out of the superior-subordinate paradigm. In AEquacy, learning to partner with others is vital;

d. **Continuous Learning** becomes a state of mind in aequal organizations. Procedures, processes, products and services, as well as people, all go through cycles of renewal, improvement, and evolution.

3) **Smart Systems** to reinforce the expected working practices of the organization and to simplify the lives of the teams and keep bureaucracy out of sight. Each organization will rethink its systems based on the AEquacy framework and its own needs, but we believe that implementing a few such systems will make the difference:

"management or operational systems"

a. Radical simplicity as an approach in the design of any system will make sure that the company doesn't fall back into the trap of bureaucracy;

b. Consent decision-making will make the decision-making process faster and provide better alignment among team members;

c. Peer feedback loops will replace the outdated Performance Management System and will give people real time, public input on how they are doing and what their next learning edge should be;

d. Information free-flow will keep people on the right page and give them the opportunity to increase innovation, to better address any issue, and to focus on what really matters instead of speculating about missing information.

4) Individual and Team Mastery must be developed, as AEquacy questions all the deeply held paradigms on how to achieve good performance in a hierarchical organization. Each individual needs to become more psychologically mature and to develop certain skills to be successful in an aequal organization:

a. Developing **Personal Mastery** is the key to finding one's own personal compass in a complex and ambiguous environment. Learning to exercise **autonomy** effectively requires both courage and empathy, so that one can reach one's goals without undermining the achievements of others;

b. **System Awareness** means developing a broader view of one's own team dynamics but also the network of dynamics of the whole organization, in order to effectively navigate and influence the system.

c. Being part of a self-organizing company means that **collaboration** is a key competence for any member. Learning to listen, engaging in productive dialogue and addressing conflict are indispensable skills for high performance.

d. **Team management** means that every person in the organization is co-accountable for the governance of the team and for the functions that were once the domain of a manager, such as hiring, planning, strategizing, and controlling. It is a whole new mindset shift.

Adopting AEquacy equips small and large organizations to better tackle complexity, to increase agility, to foster innovation, and to respond much more rapidly to internal and external challenges

AEquacy revolutionizes all the key attributes and practices of the hierarchical model:

From hierarchy	To AEquacy
Subordination	Equality
Leadership	Partnership
Control	Trust
Bureaucracy	Radically simplified systems and processes
Silos	Inter- and intra-team collaboration
Information hoarding	Transparency
Top-down strategic decision-making	Decision-making everywhere
Job titles	Dynamic roles and responsibilities
Performance reviews	Peer feedback loops
Cycle of yearly strategy-implementation	Iterative prototyping
Managers supervise and lead teams	Teams self-organize
Focus on customers	Focus on all stakeholders

Benefits of AEquacy

AGILITY: Systems are made radically simple and members of the organization are trusted to act in the best interests of the organization.

SPEED: Teams respond to market opportunities and issues rapidly, because they don't need to wait for the chain of command to take action; peer pressure and adherence to the organizational Purpose and Values are the compass for decision-making.

COLLABORATION: Teams spontaneously collaborate in the absence of department boundaries.

INNOVATION: Each team feels free to be creative to improve its P&L and its financial rewards.

PERFORMANCE: Financial and operational performance are potentially maximized through a self-balancing system that leverages the potential of each individual team.

Associates experience higher levels of engagement and personal fulfillment, greater autonomy, and an expanded sense of purpose.

In the following four Chapters we will explore all of the elements of the AEquacy framework.

I am not sure how I feel abt decision making at team level bc I worry abt coordination blw teams whose decisions affect each other. "System Awareness" is one foundational skill listed, but is the skill enough to raise consciousness of an employee to make decisions considering the whole / impacts on others

The Chapter in a nutshell

- In the last few decades, leaders have been witnessing increasing complexity and an exponential rate of change from the outside and they have experienced a number of internal challenges hindering the performance of their organizations: these include a silo mentality, rigidity, stultifying bureaucracy, an excess of systems and processes, and an outdated command & control management style.

- These challenges are common to all corporations, across geography, industries, and size, and they are all addressed in a similar fashion: by implementing technical solutions rather than challenging the whole paradigm underlying the hierarchical organizational structure.

- Even in flat pyramids, the mere presence of subordination (a few leaders who can take decisions which the rest of the employees are expected to execute) and the presence of strict control mechanisms create typical dysfunctional dynamics and behaviors that work on a system level, often unacknowledged.

- Our research shows that a good portion of both top executives and employees desire a radical change in the way the organization works. They envision a purpose-driven business with certain main keys to success: self-organizing teams, decentralized decision-making based on values and principles, and transparency.

- Based on our research, we propose a leaderless organizational design and operating system, based on a framework encompassing: 1) an Enabling Context; 2) Supporting Values; 3) Smart Systems; 4) Individual and Team Mastery. This design changes the paradigm of the traditional, hierarchical organization and paves the way for greater innovation, collaboration, and performance.

2 - ENABLING CONTEXT

From tottering on the iceberg to excelling in the ocean

[handwritten: I complicate this lens co-consts. Lens]

As we have seen in the first Chapter of the book, the current organizational paradigm – based on hierarchy, functions, and divisions – is deeply flawed. It is hard to implement real collaboration, accountability, and engagement within a system that by definition is set to create contrasting forces. It would be like pulling a rubber band and hoping that it would stay stretched after you release it.

AEquacy, on the other hand, aims to achieve a radical shift in the way companies are structured and function, and to create conditions in which all employees have a real opportunity to fully express their potential and maximize the results they generate for their organization. *[handwritten: rational problem solving to select fx of coment system]*

In the first Chapter we explained how the context in which people work influences to a large extent their behavior and, more specifically, how employees in organizations respond to the conditions determined by their hierarchical or psychological status of Bottom, Middle, and Top. We also highlighted how the

[handwritten: role/action | outcome / value]

hierarchical system actually triggers the very same dynamics that most of today's organizations are trying to dismantle.

The truth is that hierarchy creates very strong limits to what organizations can do to change their culture, their ability to be innovative and agile, and the way their people feel about and relate to their work.

As Miles Graham, former President and COO of John Hardy, eloquently put it: "Hierarchy creates frustration and doesn't reflect what people want."

During the process that led us to create the AEquacy model, we worked very hard to identify an alternative context that would represent a totally different experience for people working in an organizational setting, which would be able to enable and accelerate positive change – as opposed to derailing it, as hierarchy has been shown to do.

We asked ourselves what sort of components would be able to catalyze such a fundamental shift and we came up with four elements in particular, which we briefly introduced in the previous Chapter:

- Self-Organizing Teams
- Peer-based Coordination
- Distributed Authority
- Extended Financial Responsibility

Replacing the derailing elements embedded in the hierarchical model with the above catalysts of the AEquacy structure creates a whole new set of conditions, which inform and influence new and more productive behaviors and provide access to a whole new spectrum of previously unimagined possibilities.

To use a metaphor, having people operate within an aequal context would be like taking a penguin that has lived all its life on top of an iceberg and moving it into the open water for the very first time.

When they are not in the water, where they have exceptional swimming skills, penguins don't walk so as much as waddle, as their legs are somehow too short for a comfortable stride. Their whole body tips sideways onto one foot and then sideways again onto the other, their wings sometimes gesticulating to maintain balance. The context of hierarchy, to which we have been subjugated thus far, has forced us to mostly totter around awkwardly.

Allowing a penguin to be in its natural element, the water, completely changes its external conditions, allowing a new-found freedom and ease of movement. What possibilities could this new context enable? The aequal structure is intended to create for employees the possibility to fully express their power and abilities, exactly as a penguin would do in the water.

Of course, the transition to AEquacy may pose different challenges for people and organizations that until now have conformed to the hierarchical paradigm. In fact, the transition would require that every single person involved is able to profoundly shift their mindset about how they see themselves within the context of their organization and to prepare themselves to take on a level of accountability that they probably never experienced before.

Let's look at each one of the four elements of the AEquacy Enabling Context in more detail.

Self-Organizing Teams

Laura Donnini, Managing Director HarperCollins Italia, shared her thoughts with us: *"The world has changed. Digital technologies create the space for new decentralized organizations that function like starfish, where each arm has the ability to feed itself, move, and regenerate. When we look at decentralized organizations, there is no clearly identified leader, there are no hierarchies, nor headquarters. In this kind of structure each unit is autonomous by definition, communicates directly with other units without filters; power and knowledge are distributed and the organization is extremely fluid, able to react promptly to internal*

"First among equals"

and external stimuli without waiting for a boss's approval. In this new structure the role of the CEO transforms into a Chief Catalyst Officer, or a 'primus inter pares', who is capable of embodying and supporting values and culture to ensure that autonomous entities move in a consistent way, albeit independently, toward the achievement of the common objective."[8]

Decentralized structures, such as the sort Laura is describing, may operate as self-organizing, self-managing, or self-directing entities.

Although in the literature these have some important traits in common, and in some cases they are considered synonyms, for us it is important to draw some distinctions nonetheless. Especially when it comes to applying these concepts to business teams operating within the broader context of their organization.

Generally speaking:

A self-managed team is a team that holds a good level of autonomy; however, its goals are defined from above while the team can determine its own strategies to achieve them. This type of team still depends on an external authority, which also influences its decision-making processes.

A self-directed team has a stronger level of autonomy compared to self-managed teams, be it with reference to setting objectives and strategies or decision making. Self-directed teams are still operating within a hierarchical paradigm, however. Although they enjoy a high degree of freedom they continue to be impacted by the rules, policies, and corporate strategies of the larger organizational system.

A self-organizing team is a team where team members define their objectives, their strategies, and what roles they need. They have full decision-making autonomy and interact with other teams and with the broader organizational context through a peer-based system and a shared set of principles and values. Since there is

---

8 Reference to *The Starfish and the Spider: The Unstoppable Power of Leaderless Organizations* by Ori Brafman and Rod A. Beckstrom.

no formal leadership, there is also no hierarchical pressure on them.

Examples of successful implementation of the first two models are Semco (a portfolio management company that supports corporations that want to expand their business in Brazil), Morning Star (the world largest tomato processor), Zappos (on-line shoe and clothing store owned by Amazon), Gore (the famous waterproof and windproof clothing brand), Barry-Wehmiller (global supplier of manufacturing technology), FAVI (producer of pressure die casting, for the automotive, water, electrical, aeronautic, lock, and sanitary industries) and Buurtzorg (main home-care organization in Holland), among many others.

In these examples, hardly anyone in these organizations has a title, workers are empowered to make decisions without formal approval of a boss, and teams enjoy a very high level of autonomy, although hierarchy is always present in some kind of shape or fashion.

The AEquacy model leverages many of these concepts within a hierarchy-free environment built around self-organizing teams.

Wikipedia defines self-organization as "a process where some form of overall order arises from local interactions between parts of an initially disordered system. The process is spontaneous, not needing control by any external agent. It is often amplified by positive feedback. The resulting organization is wholly decentralized, distributed over all the components of the system. As such, the organization is typically robust and able to survive or self-repair substantial perturbation." In AEquacy, the self-organizing empowered teams are not directed and controlled from the top; rather, they are based on a network of peer relationships, where nobody has power over others and where all feel truly accountable and empowered in contributing to the team and organizational results.

The potential benefits of self-organizing teams touch many levels. The decentralization of decision-making can improve quality and speed of response to any situation and the autonomy of the teams creates a more fertile ground for innovation. These elements seem to address some key concerns of the CEOs that we have interviewed:

"One of a CEO's main challenges is being clear on what it is that makes you successful long-term but also preparing yourself for a world that you know will continue to change. And unless you understand how to change in that environment you will not win." Søren Hagh, CEO of Heineken Italy.

"I personally believe that in the future flexibility will represent one of the key challenges. We have to create an organization where you can move faster in different kinds of organizational combinations." Georg Schroeckenfuchs, CEO of Novartis Italy.

The new context created by the AEquacy structure sparks true empowerment and accountability through a high level of individual and team autonomy, both of which in turn boost employee motivation. The alignment between the individual purpose and the purpose of the organization creates the conditions for a much higher level of engagement and ownership. As a consequence, people can be more productive, committed, and motivated.

In addition, the aequal system is based on the development of an environment of continuous learning, one of the key values of AEquacy, with the view to achieving individual and team mastery.

Interestingly autonomy, mastery, and purpose are the three pillars that Daniel Pink, author of the best-selling book Drive, identifies as the best enablers of intrinsic motivation, which is what drives, engages, and stimulates people to do their best at work (the difference between intrinsic and extrinsic motivation is that whereas the latter occurs when we are motivated to perform a behavior or engage in an activity to earn a reward or avoid punishment – typical traits of a hierarchical system – the former involves engaging in a behavior because it is personally gratifying).

As Hugh O'Byrne, former VP Global Sales Center Excellence, Digital Business group at IBM, comments: *"Take millennials...they want to be trained, to know that there is a vision and purpose and they want a say in the business. That's completely at odds with the command and control structure in many companies."*

Although the actual network configuration of teams may vary from organization to organization, depending on what makes more sense and seems effective in any given context, the radial structure of AEquacy is based on specific types of teams, which represent its building blocks:

- Source Team
- Operational Team
- Coordination Team
- Service Team
- Project Team

Before looking into each type of team more specifically we need to take a small detour and explore some of the roles that we always find in each team, regardless of which type of team we are referring to. These are called Elected Roles. yes, what does a self organized team need?

Elected Roles: Coach, Meeting Host, Connectors

Although in AEquacy most roles are created by the teams based on what each team needs, there are certain roles that must always be present in order to allow the parts of the aequal system to work and interact properly.

Such roles are the Coach, the Meeting Host, and the Connectors.

✕ Coach

In general the role of the Coach is commonly seen today as that of an accelerator of growth and change, both in the form of external coaching provided by professional coaches and internal coaching provided by trained employees. We have also witnessed increasing investment by a very large number of organizations in supporting their managers to develop coaching skills, under the premise that a more coaching-oriented management style better fits what is needed today in business to manage employees.

AEquacy accelerates this trend dramatically, based on the belief that a consistent and widespread use of coaches in organizations can yield even more positive benefits. Moreover, by providing each person in the organization with some ability to operate as a coach when needed, there is an opportunity to boost the conditions to create a real learning organization.

In AEquacy, the general purpose of the Coach is to support the development of the team and to facilitate the different types of meetings a team may have, namely governance meetings or operational meetings. At the end of each meeting the team elects a Coach for the meeting that follows; the Coach can therefore change each time the team meets.

Facilitator The Coach has no official authority whatsoever over the team and its decisions; his/her role is to let the team make its own choices, even when the Coach believes there might be a better solution.

The typical operating modality of the Coach is to ask insightful questions, mirroring what he/she sees as the meeting occurs and helping to frame issues and solutions that will move the team forward. The Coach also allows the team to reflect on the dynamics the team creates as it meets, with a view to maintaining the team on an ongoing path of self-development.

Some of the characteristics that associates develop as Coaches are:

Critical thinking?
Systematic questioning.
- The ability to ask effective questions, which foster alignment, clarity, awareness, growth, and forward movement

Constructive list listening
- The ability to step into a deeper listening mode, which limits judgment and bias and promotes much more focused and constructive interactions

paraphrasing!
active listening
- The ability to focus and to summarize key points
- A "helicopter view," which brings in the external perspective that is needed to maximize creative

mind to process in big picture

thinking and innovation

empathy • Openness and empathy, which create trust and deeper bonds

Meeting Host

The general purpose of the Meeting Host is to support the logistics and organization of the meeting and make sure that the governance and operational meetings happen in line with the Team Charter and the Guiding Principles of the organization.

As with the Coach, the Meeting Host is also a role assigned by the team at the end of each meeting for the meeting that follows.

The Meeting Host is also responsible for scheduling the Operational and Governance Meetings and, at the end of each meeting, for summarizing and publishing on the AEquacy collaboration platform (an on-line environment that supports people's work in an aequal environment) the key elements of the discussions held during the meeting, the main decisions made, and the key outcomes. *rarely will people look at meeting notes...*

Hence, the role of the Meeting Host is crucial before the meeting, during the meeting, and after the meeting:

- Before the meeting – ensure that notice of the meeting is given to all participants, that a suitable location is booked and that any pre-reading that needs to be done prior to the meeting is circulated.
- During the meeting – ensure that the topics discussed during the meeting and the way the meeting develops are aligned with the Team Charter and the Guiding Principles; take notes on key points discussed, proposals and decisions made, and action points agreed.
- After the meeting – finalize the minutes from the meeting and upload them on the team's repository.

Connectors

Since AEquacy is based on teams that have a high degree of autonomy within a network of relationships and connections, it becomes clear that in order to form and maintain such interrelations the system needs people moving around and pro-actively making links between different parts and for the benefit of the whole.

In AEquacy we have three types of connectors:

- **Rep-Link** – delegate of a specific team that attends the governance and operational meetings of other connected teams that discuss topics or decisions that may impact his/her team of origin. Rep-Links have the right to intervene during such meetings and vote based on the interests of their own team.

- **Tune-Link** – delegate of a specific team that attends the governance meetings of other connected teams that may be impacted by the decisions of his/her team of origin. Tune-Links make sure that potential effects on the impacted team(s) are integrated into the relevant decision-making process of their own team.

- **Cross-Link** – delegate of a specific team that attends the operational meetings of other connected teams with a view to creating alignment and cross-pollination. Cross-Links do not have voting rights in these meetings but can advise and provide guidance as needed.

As envisioned, Coaches, Meeting Hosts, and Connectors are the elected roles that are embedded in the aequal design. In addition to these roles each team is free to define and assign different additional roles based on what they need to accomplish their goals. As a rule of thumb, in order to create the best conditions for team performance, normally teams should have a maximum number of 12 team members; beyond this number a new team should be set up.

It's now time to go deeper into the possible different types of teams that we can find in AEquacy, how they interact with each other, and how they organize their work.

*Self org. teams set their own goals/priorities, strategies for meeting them &
roles/rules, based on shared principles. Evolves &*

Types of Teams

*Gives autonomy, constant learning, & purpose, Role shin
mastery   team.*

All the teams that we can find in AEquacy share certain commonalities while maintaining their own particular attributes. In particular all teams abide by the organization's Guiding Principles and set of shared values and each member may cover different roles, including those of Rep-Links, Tune-Links, and Cross-Links, which we introduced in the previous section.

That said, each type of team also has specific characteristics.

Source Team

The Source Team is represented by the CEO and/or the original "Founders" of the organization, the CFO, all those with legal responsibilities as required by law and any other persons in the organization who have been elected by their own teams by virtue of their specific expertise or deep knowledge about the organization and its operations.

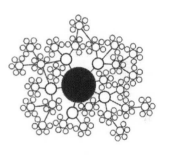

Although members of the Source Team may also be part of other types of teams and/or attend some of their specific activities, they never hold hierarchical power over others and their role is to support, coach, facilitate, and advise teams to make sure these operate in line with the organization's overall purpose and shared values.

The function of the Source Team is to define the overall purpose of the organization and to support all teams to work effectively. The Source Team is also involved in peer coordination, with a representative in each Coordination Team, and in mediating potential conflicts of role or scope between teams if the teams cannot find a resolution between themselves.

The Source Team is also responsible for designing the organization's Guiding Principles, in the case of a new company being set up (NewCo); or for involving all associates, or a representative sample of them in a very large organization, in the establishment of a Project Team with this particular objective, in the case of an existing organization transitioning to the AEquacy structure. The key concept here is that in the absence of hierarchy it is important that the associates feel that they have contributed to the output of the exercise.

The set of shared values, on the other hand, is partially pre-defined in the AEquacy model (see Chapter on Supporting Values).

In the case of a NewCo, the Source Team may also define the first teams and assign the initial members; otherwise, for an existing organization going aequal, a similar participative process to that described above is put in place for the initial set-up of the AEquacy structure.

The idea of potentially assigning these key tasks to ad-hoc Project Teams is to have a more inclusive approach in areas that touch the whole organization and leverage the contribution of many.

Operational Teams

Unlike what happens in traditional organizations, where a proliferation of staff functions has moved power and accountability away from the lines of business, in AEquacy most of the supporting tasks and responsibilities are integrated in Operational Teams, with the result of providing the latter with more autonomy and empowerment.

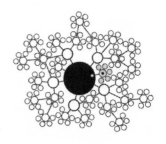

The scope of each Operational Team is to serve external clients, directly or indirectly, and each Operational Team may operate autonomously to achieve its own objectives in line with the principles that we have presented so far.

Normally this type of team does not have a pre-determined duration and its life cycle ends when its specific purpose no longer makes sense for its team members and the organization (in which case team members volunteer to be assigned to other teams).

Examples of Operational Teams are a customer service team for a specific product, a production team in charge of assembling a product, a design team that is implementing an app for a client, a team of sales representatives or consultants selling products or services of the organization, etc.

Coordination Team

Their scope is to maintain coherence in the projects and activities of the teams they coordinate vis-à-vis the purpose and values of the organization.

We would like to reiterate that in the AEquacy system, "Coordination" teams are not intended as entities with power over others, but rather as entities that serve to harmonize and bring together the work of the different teams connected to them. Hence, their presence does not introduce any form of hierarchy whatsoever.

Coordination teams may create and/or revise the purpose of the teams they coordinate and are formed by a Rep-Link of each coordinated team and a Tune-link from the Source Team. Given that the Coordination team is made up of peers who are representatives of the connected teams, this effectively means that colleagues from the various interconnected teams meet and self-coordinate themselves.

One important responsibility of Coordination Teams is to

process in their Governance Meetings any source of entropy that may arise as a consequence of the teams' daily activities. As we saw in the first chapter, entropy in this case can be defined as the amount of energy that is wasted within the system as a consequence of behaviors that are driven by potentially limiting values.

Another important task of Coordination Teams is to assess whether the aggregated financials of the associated teams are sustainable and, should this not be the case, to provide guidance and feedback until a more healthy balance is achieved.

Coordination Teams may emerge from an Operational Team when its size gets too big and its operations start to be differentiated and assigned to newly formed Operational Teams. Conversely, a Coordination Team ends when the associated Operational Teams cease to exist or collapse back into the original team they came from.

An example of a Coordination Team is one that harmonizes the activities of several operational teams working on the same product or service, or one that coordinates all the operational teams dedicated to various communication activities (i.e. advertising, website, social media, public relations, etc.).

Service Teams

Service Teams are created by the Source Team and/or the Coordination Teams, depending on specific shared needs that may arise from other teams, which could be addressed by an external service.

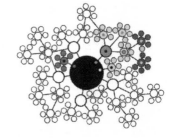

The scope of a Service Team is therefore to support and facilitate the work of their internal clients (other teams) with the highest standards and in the most effective way.

A specific Service Team exists so long as its purpose has

[handwritten: meaning! yes   we want our work to matter ☆]

meaning for its team members and the supported teams.

An example of a Service Team is one organizing events for all or a subset of Operational teams; or one providing Research & Development services for a specific line of products.

Also, Service Teams have their own P&L, as their services are effectively sold to their internal clients.

[handwritten: ↳ ? profit / loss   how to calculate ?]

Project Teams

A Project Team may be created based on the emerging needs of any other type of team, which also sets the Project Team's purpose and appoints its initial members.

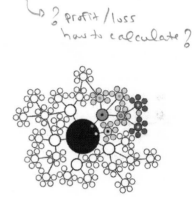

The scope of Project Teams is to achieve specific, time-bound objectives, and they are dissolved once the expected results are achieved.

The activities of the Project Teams can vary significantly depending on what the organization and the other types of teams need at any given moment in time. Examples of Project Teams are a team tasked to design the process to define the company's Guiding Principles, a team that has been assigned to resolve a specific organizational issue, or a team that has to assess the feasibility of a specific initiative that is going to be launched.

Relationships between teams

"The old ways of creating relationships don't work anymore, they must be more fluid. In the organization we want to allow the system to see, heal and repair itself.. this must now happen to 6,000 of us." – Phil Clothier, Chief Executive Officer, Barrett Values Centre

As stated earlier, creating self-organizing teams can yield a number of benefits only if such teams are interacting within a broader system that is able to create and maintain a healthy balance among its components.

In a context where every team enjoys a high level of autonomy, the actual intelligence of the system is determined by the pathways of connections and interrelations that form the relationships between the teams.

info-flow Through such relationships, information is shared, resources *resource* are allocated more effectively, innovation flows, meaningful *alloc.* collaboration occurs, and ultimately decisions are made more *Innovation* quickly and in line with a common higher purpose.

collaboration The underlying logic is that the more access people have to one another, the more possibilities there are. Without connections, nothing happens. With AEquacy, people have access to everyone and the different resources available anywhere in the organization to accomplish what they need to accomplish.

 In other words, higher effectiveness, speed, and performance are created by letting people freely access the collective intelligence of the system. Without boundaries and without unnecessary limitations.

There are different ways aequal Teams interact with each other. One key role in this respect is played out by the Connectors, namely, Rep-Links, Tune-Links, and Cross-Links. If on the one hand, these roles are necessary to guarantee a certain balance in the system, as we have seen, on the other hand they all represent a crucial resource that connects different teams and shares key information as needed.

Another way Teams can interact is through the AEquacy Collaboration Platform, or similar advanced collaboration tools. Many organizations today are implementing systems that combine tools and processes to ensure that employees can connect with the people, information, and resources they require at any given time. The AEquacy platform integrates these features and many more in order to create within the organization an environment that reproduces the actual radial structure of the firm as it evolves and provides the associates with all they need to leverage the resources available and run their operations in line with the AEquacy principles.

How aequal teams operate

In the hierarchical paradigm, traditionally, a manager decides and employees execute, whereas in the new AEquacy paradigm individuals and teams are required to make their own decisions. This creates a fundamental shift in the conditions under which people operate: individuals no longer feel used and unheard and instead start to take ownership. Working in a hierarchy-free environment, however, poses certain challenges, especially when it comes to re-thinking the way people should work and interact with one another.

Such an environment is very different compared to the team setting of a traditional organization, as here people are driven by a common purpose and are fully accountable for defining objectives and strategies, as well as for managing any issue or challenge that may emerge. Some may find this new level of autonomy inspiring and stretching, while others may find it uncomfortable and frightening since, in a way, there are no more excuses for avoiding ownership and accountability.

As an example, in a traditional team structure, conflicts can escalate to the point that a manager needs to step in and resolve them. Self-organized teams, in contrast, must identify different ways to find and address any day-to-day conflicts (see Chapter Four on Smart Systems for more details on this).

Another important element that differentiates how aequal teams work, as opposed to teams in traditional organizations, is that team members come together primarily in two types of meetings, namely governance meetings and operational meetings, the duration of which is established in advance by participants. Governance meetings are aimed at determining how the team is governed in terms of roles, responsibilities, and guidelines, whereas in operational meetings, teams solve issues related to their projects and discuss their progress vis-à-vis their OKRs

Salvation – teams of scientists

(Objectives and Key Results), which we explain in more detail in the following sections. Additional meetings can be set up directly by team members (from the same team or across different teams) any time they deem it useful, but even in this case only the relevant stakeholders are invited.

What we often hear from our clients is that the "abuse" and "spread" of ineffective meetings is taking a toll on everybody's ability to get things done. According to an article recently published by Harvard Business Review[9] based on interviews with 182 senior managers in a range of industries: "65% said meetings keep them from completing their own work. 71% said meetings are unproductive and inefficient. 64% said meetings come at the expense of deep thinking. 62% said meetings miss opportunities to bring the team closer together."

By dramatically simplifying the types of meetings that people have and using them to discuss what really matters for the team and for the organization, the AEquacy system may resolve this most lamented plague of today's organizations.

Let's take a step back now…in order to understand how aequal teams contribute to the broader organizational system and work. It is worth making a distinction between purpose, objectives & results, and strategy.

Purpose

An organization's purpose is the reason why it exists, beyond the profit. It answers the question "Why is our existence important?" or "What difference do we make in the world?" and it must be meaningful and inspirational for all members. The purpose is broad in scope and it is written succinctly for everyone to remember and to make it simple to use as a compass in people's daily operations. Daniel Pink defines individual purpose as the desire to do something that has meaning and is important.

---

9 *"Stop the Meeting Madness"* by Leslie A. Perlow, Constance Noonan Hadley, Eunice Eun, *HBR*, July-August 2017.

The overall company purpose is defined by the Source Team, which also defines the purpose of the teams that radiate directly from it. Likewise, each team that creates new teams defines their purpose.

This process allows consistency across the system and sets a clear direction for the whole organization as well as its sub-elements.

Each individual is also required to set his or her own purpose in line with two simple criteria: it has to be consistent with their team's purpose and it must be meaningful at a personal level. This ensures alignment at all levels and boosts individual engagement.

According to Fortune, the best workplaces for millennials moving forward will be those where they will be able to connect to their work and feel part of something significant.

As Magda Mook, CEO/Executive Director at International Coach Federation (ICF), puts it: "*I think that part of the reason why people are so disengaged from their work is that they don't understand how they belong, they don't understand the system, all they know is their little bubble that they're living within and they don't understand how they contribute to the good of the organization.*"

As advertised by the Conscious Capitalism movement, conscious businesses focus on their purpose beyond profit, and by focusing on a deeper purpose, a conscious business inspires, engages, and energizes its stakeholders.

Objectives and Key Results (OKRs)

The OKR framework is a simple approach to creating alignment and engagement around measurable goals. Introduced by John Doerr in 1999, this approach is currently being adopted by an increasing number of successful and innovative organizations, such as Google, Intel, Oracle, Sears Holding Corp., Hobsons, and many others.

Within AEquacy, each team defines its own objectives

coherently with its assigned purpose. Since the aequal operating system is based on the notion of radical simplicity, aequal teams only focus on one (maximum two) relevant and stretching objective, which in turn drives the definition of the Key Results and the team's strategies. As with any other piece of information, the OKRs of each team are also openly shared and accessible within the organization.

According to the OKR framework, objectives answer the question: "What do we want to achieve?" and are normally defined in qualitative terms. Furthermore they must be relevant for the whole organization, consistent with the team's purpose, and must inspire the team members. An example could be: "Build an affordable and safe flying car in 3 years."

On the other hand, key results answer the question: "How will we know that we have succeeded and reached our objective?" and must be expressed in measurable terms. Normally for each objective there should be two or three solid key results.

Building on the previous example, some possible key results could be: "Test the first prototype in the next 12 months", "Keep the total cost of the prototype to €150,000" and "Have no mechanical failures while testing the prototype".

The team's OKRs also drive the individual team members' OKRs, which should be consistent and represent a significant contribution to the team's OKRs. The individual OKRs are shared with the rest of the organization, as well.

Each team is responsible for reviewing their OKRs vis-à-vis the results achieved and using these conversations as a basis to raise the bar and improve in the future.

Strategy

The Oxford dictionary defines Strategy as "a plan of action designed to achieve a long-term or overall aim", which in the traditional organization normally translates into an annual plan to achieve the business objectives (financial but not only) of the different divisions.

This approach typically provides very few opportunities to discuss strategy decisions throughout the year; outside of these fixed windows, strategy is rarely discussed and, as a result, the strategy becomes too rigid and the process for adjusting it is inefficient. Worryingly, this happens in a world where big changes in market conditions and technological disruptions happen at a rate that can be far more frequent than the traditional 12-month period that normally lapses before the creation of a new strategy. The last 30 years are filled with examples of companies that went from being market leaders to simply disappearing because of their strategic inertia: Kodak, Motorola, Nokia, TWA, and Texaco, to name a few.

It should not surprise us that, according to HBR,[10] 75% of organizations today struggle to implement a strategy, due to a number of additional factors such as lack of cooperation across teams, a rigidity in handling changing external conditions, a lack of true alignment on and shared understanding of key strategic priorities, an (almost) exclusive focus on numbers, and strategy driven from the top.

Research[11] suggests that moving the focus from the annual strategic plan to a policy of seizing ongoing strategic opportunities, while coordinating across the company and adjusting as needed, may be a much more effective way to look at strategy.

While adopting this perspective may represent a huge shift for traditional hierarchical organizations, it is a naturally embedded cultural element in AEquacy. Here teams are fully empowered to determine the best strategies that will allow them to achieve their OKRs. In the AEquacy paradigm the definition of strategy evolves within the context of an uncertain and rapidly changing environment, where prediction is no longer a meaningful activity and the ability to create adaptive plans becomes a key success

---

10 "Why Strategy Execution Unravels—and What to Do About It", *HBR*, October 2016.
11 *Always-On Strategy* by Nicolas Kachaner and Peter Kunnas, Boston Consulting Group, April 2017.

If operational teams are determining their own Coordinated
Strategies does that provide problems of coordination?

factor.

Søren Hagh, CEO of Heineken Italy, shared with us that *"The biggest risk for a job like mine is always that information travels through many layers before it gets to you and the performance in the market is very often one of the most lacking indicators, so unless you pick up issues way before they materialize in terms of negative business results, then it would be too late."*

In the AEquacy system, associates become designers as well as executors of their team strategies. They are also entitled to suggest, during their operational meetings, changes in strategies to their teams, should they devise ways to increase the speed and impact of execution of the team vis-à-vis their OKRs. As a consequence the level of commitment and engagement is much higher compared to that found in traditional hierarchical organizations.

Peer-based coordination

Interestingly, there is very little literature about peer-based coordination, let alone a clear definition of what it means. Our assumption is that so little has been written about it because this concept is simply not compatible with a world where the vast majority of organizations are based on a vertical power structure, which inevitably exists within the paradigm of top-down coordination.

The paradox is that today's technological advancements quite clearly support a transition towards a networked society that favors peer-based relationships – a society that is increasingly characterized by decentralized authority and is built around multiple and interdependent centers of decision making, a superior capacity to adapt and evolve in response to a changing environment, the free flow of information, easy access to resources, and a strong ability to innovate. And the same trend is becoming more and more evident in the business world as well.

also definition based on trust.

In fact, the peer-based organization is much more in harmony with the increasing complexity of the business environment, with people's needs and aspirations, and with human dynamics that support high performance in the workplace. Peer coordination offers companies a more efficient way to organize and manage their business, while creating a much healthier and more "human" environment for their people compared to what we would find in a typical organization built around the hierarchical paradigm. It also empowers employees to be more creative and gives them the motivation to think and act like owners.

we have a sense of what this means

The peer-based system creates an inclusive, participatory organization, where the distinction of "Top", "Middle", or "Bottom" is replaced by true equality and where each associate can contribute to the best of their ability. Needless to say, in this context the notion of "peer" does not imply that everyone in the organization is the same but rather, as Jeffrey Nielsen stated in his book The Myth of Leadership, that peer-based organizations create the conditions to achieve unity in diversity and diversity in unity, thus freeing up the real potential of the organization.

Of course a successful transition to a peer-based system is not a pain-free process, especially since most of today's companies are still fully rooted in the old hierarchical paradigm. The benefits of the peer-based system can be harvested only if certain conditions are in place.

The culture of the organization must have a certain level of readiness to embark on such a transformational journey and must be open to embracing a peer-based mindset. Most of all, the changes needed to make the transition happen must come from within the organization and not be imposed from without or from the top (which is the typical way big changes have been traditionally approached and one of the main reasons why those very same initiatives tend to fail or under-deliver).

The employees themselves need to be co-creators of the new design, as this in itself represents the very first action that exemplifies peer-based thinking. In other words, if you do not genuinely share decision-making power and authority from the very beginning of the process, you will not gain the passion and participation of the employees and, even more crucially, their trust in the process.

A peer-based organization implies by definition that there is no rank; everyone comes together as peers, and that means the CEO as well as the frontline worker. Every associate may tap into the intelligence of the system, and giving all participants input into decision making allows the best possible decisions to be made in any situation and with a level of responsiveness that is much more suited to the rapidly evolving business context. Teams and individuals become the key centers of authority and decision-making power. This creates a positive self-reinforcing mechanism whereby the more associates participate in decision making, the more their energy and engagement are reinforced. Furthermore, within a peer-based system, individuals tend to expand their range of interests beyond narrow self-interest to include a deeper concern for the well-being of the organization as a whole.

Peer-based coordination can exist only if the notion of power over someone or something is dropped from the start and everyone in the organization is fully empowered to act in the best interests of their team and of the organization. In the AEquacy system, since everyone is considered a peer, one's decisions and actions are not regulated by someone else's authority but rather by peer-pressure mechanisms that emerge directly from the system – all of which requires a strong foundation of trust.

Hierarchical organizations, however, are built around the belief that employees are not to be fully trusted and that their work has to be supervised and controlled in order to guarantee certain standards and work outputs. The consequence of this belief is that companies incur huge costs, paying managers who are tasked with controlling others, and are cluttered with control mechanisms, which in turn generate bureaucracy and inefficiencies, slowing down innovation. According to an article published in Harvard Business Review in 2011, the cost of management (referring to the salaries of middle and senior managers whose time is dedicated to supervising others) accounts in organizations for 33% of the payroll.[12] Furthermore, the impact on those who feel controlled is often demotivation, disempowerment, and disengagement from the organization.

AEquacy, on the other hand, is a manager-free and control-free system, where the equilibrium is established and maintained within teams and across teams during meetings through peer pressure and peer coordination mechanisms. The underlying belief here is that people tend to give their best when their actions are guided not by orders from someone up the chain of command but by feeling truly empowered to contribute to the team's and organization's purpose and by feeling trusted.

Since in AEquacy there is no hierarchy, eliminating managers may free up huge resources that can be used to invest in innovation, increasing the salaries of the associates so as to render the organization more attractive as an employer, or in other relevant areas.

Coordination within each team happens through the team's Charter and the organization's Guiding Principles and Supporting Values, as well as the Operational and Governance meetings. Should a team member try to take advantage of the system or fail to contribute to the team results, his or her fellow team members will provide feedback and, should the issue persist, could ultimately decide to remove this person from the team. In aequal teams no one is exempt from feedback; team members learn to tackle the elephant in the room within their team as soon as they see it and to deal with any uncomfortable issue openly, whether it be an underperforming peer, a strategy implementation issue, a missed opportunity, or a different type of tension.

---

12 "First, Let's Fire All the Managers" by Gary Hamel, *Harvard Business Review* 2011.

Distributed Authority

In their article "To Be a Better Leader, Give Up Authority",[13] authors Amar, Hentrich and Hlupic maintain that in order to be successful, organizations should abandon the traditional structure in which decision rights are reserved for people at the top and also understand that leadership is less about delegating tasks and monitoring results, than it is about imbuing the entire workforce with a sense of responsibility for the business.

Over the past two decades, the field of management has been inundated with books on leadership, and companies have invested considerable amounts in leadership training in the attempt to create a better-performing business culture. At Asterys we have been asked by our clients several times to design and deliver such programs and each engagement produced deep learning for us as well as for the participants. After many years we also came to a very important realization: no matter how well structured, innovative, or inspiring a program was, its effects in the long term would not be as transformational as we had hoped to see for our clients. The level of enthusiasm participants had at the end of our programs was always extremely high, as was their appreciation for what they had learned. However, in conversations with the same people after a few months, most would state that notwithstanding their attempts and determination to apply what they had learned with their teams, the "system" within which such attempts were made rendered most efforts to change the leadership culture of their organization in a more evolutionary and people-centric direction futile. The system which so thwarted their efforts was their hierarchy-based organization. In such an environment, where authority and power are distributed according to strict vertical rules, most of the organizational dynamics remained unaffected, no matter how "illuminated" participants in the leadership development programs had become.

The truth is that hierarchy hinders the distribution of power and

---

13 First published in *Harvard Business Review*, December 2009.

decision-making authority to those of a lower rank in the organization. In the presence of hierarchy, the underlying belief is that wisdom and the ability to make the right decisions reside primarily at the top. In fact, in traditional hierarchical companies, the organization chart and the job titles define the levels of authority. In this context hoarding information is a way to maintain one's own power, and making decisions becomes a cumbersome process characterized by bottlenecks, disempowerment, and organizational friction. Not to mention that more often than not, decisions are made based not on the best possible response to any given situation but rather on an estimated guess made by someone not directly involved with that specific situation.

In this setting, managers do not trust their subordinates to be autonomous in making the best possible decisions for their division or for the organization. And guess what: they're right! How could it be otherwise, within a context where information does not flow, is often fragmented, and more often than not is not even shared?

In the AEquacy system, in contrast, a key belief is that wisdom is distributed among all the people in the company and that all associates should therefore have the authority to make those decisions that affect their work and that they deem useful for their teams and their organization.

When employees believe that lines of authority and decision-making power are fixed and lie primarily at the top, they will not feel fully accountable in their roles and will never fully engage in their work. Furthermore, they will tend to relinquish responsibility to their superiors, where decision-making authority rests, and un-learn the ability to contribute proactively and with a more entrepreneurial spirit to the common cause.

Moreover, in the absence of distributed authority, there is rarely any honest and open communication. People who feel themselves at the "Bottom" will only tell those who they perceive as "Tops" what they think these "Tops" want to hear, whereas people who feel themselves at the "Top" will only tell those below them what they think these "Bottoms" need to know in order to execute certain tasks. These dynamics set the conditions for disempowerment and low trust, creating a huge gap between business reality and the world of the Tops – which, by the way, is a plague that has hit nearly every large organization that we have come across. Interestingly, rather than trying to close this dangerous gap by improving communication flows and bringing decision-making power to the front line, the most common action that companies take to address the issue is to implement even stricter control mechanisms. Needless to say, this line of action does nothing but reinforce and perpetuate the very same issue it is trying to fix.

The most advanced organizations, on the other hand, have learnt that the most effective decision-making often happens when the right to make decisions is granted to those closest to the problem. This works if there is trust that people working in the organization will act in the best interests of the company and if all information can be accessed freely whenever someone in the organization needs it.

Thomas Malone, a professor at the MIT Sloan School of Management, says that the cheap cost of communication, be it e-mail, instant messaging or the Internet in general, is making possible a new type of decentralized organizational structure, characterized by the "participation of people in making the decisions that matter to them", which really means distributing authority to all employees.

By distributing authority, aequal organizations put power in the hands of those best positioned to find the right solution. In the aequal environment, people and teams can access any resource they may need to make the right decisions quickly. *Can they?*

Distributed authority also means shifting the responsibility into the hands of every single associate, who takes ownership to resolve issues as issues present themselves. If the issue is too big or systemic each associate can propose the creation of a Project Team tasked with analyzing and resolving the issue.

→ how to reduce repeat / or consolidate "info / research"

information is not the only consideration in dialogue decision making.

authority comes out of relationship

Of course, as stated before, the goal here is to optimize the decision-making process by virtue of distributed authority both among aequal teams and to each individual in the organization, AND to do so within a larger system that has the ability to maintain balance despite the substantial decentralization of decisions. The way this is achieved is, once again, through the presence of specific roles (Rep-Links and Cross-Links) in the various governance or operational meetings, where decisions are validated through the consent process (see Chapter Four on Smart Systems). This method preserves the autonomy of the decision maker while assuring that the decision being made does not negatively affect other teams and/or the larger organization.

Furthermore, should the particular aequal structure include Coordination Teams, these also become the venue where specific decisions can be discussed and be subject to the consent-based process.

Moving from hierarchy and centralized decision-making power to peer-based coordination and decentralized authority allows everyone to find their unique talents and make their authentic contribution to the organization.

Extended financial responsibility

Generally speaking, every year all organizations invest time and resources in running a budgeting exercise, which is supposed to create the best possible estimate of what the company will earn, spend, and invest in the coming year.

The reality is that this exercise, which is designed purely to predict and control, often proves to be inaccurate, time-consuming, subject to manipulation, and excessively numbers-driven. Moreover, it frequently ignites conflicts and political games between different parts of the organization and between the organization and the shareholders. Let's explore some of these flaws in greater detail.

Budgets are by definition inaccurate, since they are built on a long list of assumptions in estimating revenues and expenses and on the information available at the time the budget is created. In a world where the speed of change is skyrocketing it's easy to see how quickly any forecast created on such ground may soon prove outdated and therefore unreliable. Any unanticipated shift in the market conditions could easily impact in a significant way on any budgeted number. And the likelihood that this will happen is quite high.

Budgeting is time-consuming and rigid. A lot of resources and time are allocated to the attempt to make the estimates as accurate as possible, especially in large organizations where the corporate budget is the result of many budgeting processes that happen at a divisional or functional level. Furthermore, given the huge effort that normally goes into the yearly budgeting exercise, budgets tend to be rigid, meaning that their numbers tend to be fixed and don't "react" to external changes that may occur.

Budgets are subject to manipulation. Budgeting is normally a top-down exercise and typically includes very challenging, often unrealistic, revenue forecasts and strong pressure to set costs low to preserve high margins for shareholders. This may easily foster defensive mechanisms at a divisional or functional level; for example, managers may react by deliberately inflating their expenses and reducing their revenue targets, with a view to "demonstrating" at the end of the year how good they were in incurring lower costs and achieving higher revenues than had been budgeted upfront. In other situations, this mechanism creates another interesting dynamic, whereby managers spend all the funds allocated in their own budget under the belief that if they do not use as much as they are authorized to spend in the current year, the funds budgeted to them in the next period will be reduced. Of course this often results in a non-efficient use of the funds available, to the detriment of the company's bottom line.

Budgeting is primarily financially oriented, as it focuses on the quantitative aspect of the business and addresses very marginally the more qualitative aspects of the business, including the needs of the employees and those of the customers.

Additional potential drawbacks of the budgeting process include a lack of flexibility in decision-making, excessive focus on short-term decisions to "keep within the budget", demotivation of employees due to unrealistic targets and a top-down approach, or departmental rivalry and battles over budget allocation.

Furthermore, there is a high risk that instead of creating and adapting strategies based on evolving market conditions, the Senior Management may set strategies that revolve around and are guided primarily by the budgeted numbers.

As Nicolas Kachaner and Peter Kunnas from Boston Consulting Group stated in a recent article,[14] companies will increase their odds of success in today's turbulent environment only if they learn to complement their traditional annual strategy-setting process with something more dynamic, which they call an "always-on" strategy. According to the authors, an always-on strategy gives companies a systematic way to scan for signs of disruption and explore unexpected changes to the strategic environment.

Self-organizing teams spontaneously organize themselves to cope with any external disturbance and are able to adjust their strategies in real time whenever needed, without having to get external formal approval or go through cumbersome strategy review processes.

The AEquacy model introduces the possibility of completely transcending the above dangers and inefficiencies, by replacing altogether the way an organization thinks and looks at managing its financial aspects.

In aequal organizations every team is free to craft its own budget based on what is really needed to achieve its objective for the year. There is thus no pressure from above; whatever numbers the team forecasts become the team's budget. In some

---

14 *Always-On Strategy* by Nicolas Kachaner and Peter Kunnas, Boston Consulting Group, April 2017.

cases, peers from the Coordination Teams or from the Source Team may challenge specific budgets, but no one can force a team to change their numbers so long as individual budgets as well as their aggregate make financial sense.

Throughout the year the budget is kept fluid and is seamlessly adjusted to any relevant change in the external conditions, and at the end of the year, after the team has placed a fixed percentage in the organization's common pot, the team decides how much to distribute and how to distribute it, and how much to reinvest.

In essence, in the AEquacy system the logic behind budgets dramatically shifts from being primarily a performance-control mechanism to being a key tool in making decisions and supporting the teams' operations.

Another important potential implication of adopting this latter view on managing the financials of the organization is that the way people are rewarded can be approached in a very different way as well.

Traditionally, the salary of an employee represents, broadly speaking, the cost of acquiring and retaining that specific employee and is typically determined by comparing market pay rates for people performing similar work in similar industries in the same region. Besides this general rule, in hierarchical organizations the definition of individual salaries normally follows rules and criteria that have very little to do with rewarding the actual value one creates for one's team and for the organization as a whole.

Gross inequities in pay make true community unachievable and genuine relationships impossible. Those organizations that achieve a real sense of solidarity have checks on excessive executive pay and use more team-based compensation.

In aequal organizations the issue of salary inequality is transcended, since each team defines the salaries for team members based on criteria that each team deems fair, so long as there are no major differences with the average salaries paid in

[handwritten: Can every team remain profitable & what about some team being more profitable than others?]

the rest of the organization and the team itself remains profitable.

The assumption is that associates will keep their salaries at a fair level since they are fully aware of the economic conditions of their organization and know what the market is willing to pay for them. Furthermore, if someone requests a salary or pay rise which is too high, their peers are likely to reject the request, as every salary is approved on a consent basis.

Interestingly, there are a growing number of organizations that are experimenting with ways to define salaries based on what seem to be fair principles. Examples include the Holacracy Badge-Based Compensation App and the Slicing Pie method (which has been quite successful especially with start-ups).

The former allows employees (partners in Holacracy) to define and earn "Badges", where each Badge represents a useful skill, talent, achievement, or something similarly useful for determining compensation. Partners earn a Badge by demonstrating the skill or whatever the Badge represents; thus any given set of Badges may have a specific compensation level tied to the set.

The Slicing Pie method is a formula based on the principle that a person's financial recognition should always be equal to that person's share of the at-risk contributions, which include time, money, ideas, relationships, supplies, equipment, facilities, or anything else someone provides without full payment of its fair market value. The formula translates all these elements into a meta-currency, named Slice, and each employee gets paid based on the number of Slices he/she contributes.

Matt Black Systems, a manufacturing business in the aerospace industry, based in England, demonstrated that such a radical shift in how the financial aspects of an organization are managed is not only possible, but can also generate tremendous benefits. Since they started to financially manage their organization based on principles similar to those described here, they achieved +300% in productivity, +10% in profit margins, their customer perception has shifted from poor to outstanding, product returns are at less than 1%, "on time and in full" delivery is greater than 96%, and pay has increased 100%.

Matt Black Systems employees are individually rewarded for their contribution to each product; they are not "compensated" for the hours spent at work.

Another valuable example of what is possible in this domain is provided by TMC, an international high-tech company. TMC has adopted a new model that they call "employeneurship", which has revolutionized the way work and relationships are handled in the organization and has created an environment based on ownership, responsibility, entrepreneurship, and freedom. As TMC International's CEO, Emmanuel Mottrie, has stated, the intention of this model is to create a platform that can be leveraged by their engineers to be at their best and have success. This platform is based on complete transparency, including access to all company financial information.

At TMC engineers have a fixed base salary and a variable salary that is proportionate to the value they create for the organization. Furthermore, they are all given space, money, time, and support, so they can start a new product or service or idea.

Of course, it's not our intention to dismiss the importance of having a system in place that allows the organization to manage its financials; we are simply pointing out that what has worked so far is probably outdated and not suitable to support organizations operating in the current business environment.

The Chapter in a nutshell

- Aequal organizations aim to create conditions whereby individuals and teams can express their real potential in service of the value they create for their company. This is achieved within a context that enables true empowerment and accountability and replaces the limiting conditions that are embedded in a hierarchical structure. The key elements of this enabling context are: Self-Organizing Teams, Peer-based Coordination, Distributed Authority, and Extended Financial Responsibility.

- Self-Organizing Teams are teams where team members define their objectives, their strategies, and what roles they need. They have full decision-making autonomy and interact with each other through a peer-based system and a set of principles and values. Aequal teams have strong autonomy and the overall network of teams (the organization) is kept in balance by virtue of how the AEquacy structure is built and maintained. There are elective team roles that allow the AEquacy system to work effectively: Coach, Meeting Host, and Connectors (Rep-Links, Tune-Links, and Cross-Links).

- Peer-based coordination means that everything that happens in an aequal organization happens among peers and in the absence of any type of hierarchy. Peer coordination offers companies a more efficient way to organize and manage their business, while creating a much healthier and more human environment for their people, who are freer to contribute, and to feel and act like owners of the business.

- Distributed authority has to do with making each team and each individual within the team a decision-maker, as this puts power in the hands of those best positioned to make the best possible decisions to resolve an issue or leverage an opportunity.

- Extended financial responsibility creates a radical shift in the way organizations normally handle their financial aspects.

Every team is accountable for their own P&L and decides how to handle their financial decisions so long as the peer-based advice process is honored and such decisions are in the service of the team's objectives and are coherent with the organization's purpose. The logic of managing financials to monitor and control is replaced with that of supporting the best possible decisions to support each team's operations.

3 - SUPPORTING VALUES

The trouble with organizational culture and values

Søren Hagh, CEO of Heineken Italy, shared the following insight with us: *"People don't take culture seriously. I think creating a certain culture and values in an organization doesn't come because you write it on a piece of paper or you talk about it with your investors. It comes because you live it every single day, so it starts with a total belief that culture drives the success of the business. If you think it is something you do after you've done all the rest it will not change anything. Culture, however, is less tangible. Unless you create tools to allow people to work with something that is abstract, they will not succeed. And if you don't measure it, people will not take it seriously. You measure the bottom line and you measure the market share and if you don't measure culture it will never get the same share of attention."*

We couldn't agree more with these reflections, which also mirror the findings of the Deloitte research we mentioned in the first chapter of the book, according to which cultural issues are among the top challenges business leaders are currently facing.

But what is culture anyway?

Organizational culture has been defined in a myriad of ways. It could be described for instance as the intangible human element that shapes "how things get done" or, in a more articulate way, as the sets of behaviors, values, reward systems, and rituals that make up the organization and that become evident through people's behaviors and attitudes.

In fact, culture can mean many things, and different definitions can be correct at the same time. However, one that stands out for us is the one that identifies culture as the collective value system of a specific organization.

In his book The Values-Driven Organization, Richard Barrett defines values as a "shorthand method of describing what is important to us individually or collectively at any given moment in time." He also maintains that values are not fixed, as those that are important to us at any particular moment in our lives tend to be a reflection of the needs we are experiencing in our life circumstances at that specific moment in time (in Chapter 5 we will explore in more depth the link between needs and values).

Our experience is that very often companies underestimate the importance of culture and use their values purely as a slogan rather than a way to manage their business. Enron came to symbolize a very clear example of a company that operated quite far from its officially declared values. In 2001 Enron was one of the world's major electricity, natural gas, communications, and pulp and paper companies, with claimed revenues of nearly $101 billion. Enron had also been named as "America's Most Innovative Company" for six consecutive years by Fortune. Its official values were Communication, Respect, Integrity, and Excellence.

In 2001, however, Enron also represented the largest bankruptcy in American history and became a well-known example of willful corporate fraud and corruption, as a consequence of the mismanagement and illegal practices perpetuated by its leaders for many years. In a way, Enron has become a prominent example of a company whose list of values were, at the end of the day, totally meaningless.

As Arrigo Berni, President of Moleskine, stated: *"Whether the organizational culture is healthy or dysfunctional, in my view, is very much a consequence of the quality of the leadership at all levels in that organization. Why? Because the example always comes from the top."*

The lack of serious attention to organizational culture and values is to us quite bizarre, as the separation between intangible and tangible elements in business should be long gone. The knowledge economy has taught us how intangibles like intellectual property and design can be converted into money and that tangibles and intangibles are often interchangeable.

According to an article published in Fortune magazine in March 2016 titled "Corporate Culture and the Bottom Line," there are many reasons why the matter of culture should be taken very seriously in the corporate world. One reason above all is that in doing so, not only can companies build better places to work but they can also create better conditions to fuel their bottom line. The same article reports that research by the Great Place to Work Institute over three decades has demonstrated that a positive workplace culture correlates with strong business performance. In fact, the publicly traded companies on the annual list of the 100 best workplaces outperform the S&P 500 index 3 to 1.

In most other cases, however, even when the topic of culture is on the CEO's list of priorities, it doesn't ultimately get addressed as it should. One of the reasons for this is that the value of culture is not easy to quantify, so other priorities that have a more straightforward link to the company's financials tend to be privileged, while the issue of culture keeps being postponed.

Based on a study by Gallup,[15] just 23% of US employees strongly agree that they can apply their organization's values to their work every day, and only 27% strongly agree that they "believe in" their organization's values. In a different study carried out by the Boston Research Group, called the "National Governance, Culture and Leadership Assessment" (based on a survey of thousands of American employees covering all different ranks in their organizations), only 3% declared themselves to be guided by a "set of core principles and values that inspire everyone to align around a company's mission."

One of the main reasons for this is that even when CEOs decide to pay attention to how their company's values are defined, this is usually done as a top-down exercise where the CEOs or the headquarters select values that define what they believe their ideal culture should be. As one may imagine, however, these values fail to resonate with employees or influence the way work gets done. With so few employees strongly agreeing they can apply their company's values to their work every day or believing in their company's values, most businesses need to strengthen their culture and bring their values to life.

Moreover, organizational culture develops whether or not there is a conscious effort to shape it. If it's ignored it will continue to develop – and hardly in the way one might hope. Without attention, it could easily grow in the direction of politics, fear, micromanagement, risk-aversion, short-term focus, bureaucracy, control, or silo mentality, just to name a few of the elements that were shown in Chapter 1 to determine high levels of entropy and dysfunction in today's organizations.

As Giglio del Borgo, CEO of Diners Club Italia, puts it: *"Knowing your company values and making those values live consistently – it's fundamental. In organizations often you don't find this, and as*

---

15 "Few Employees Believe in their Company's Values," Nate Dvorak and Bailey Nelson, *Gallup Business Journal*, September 2016.

a result you have silos, fear, lack of transparent interactions...with all the inauspicious consequences that this can imply."

Why are values so important, again?

Laura Donnini, CEO of HarperCollins Italia, shared that *"For the new generations the sense of community and the alignment with key principles are becoming more important than the career itself. For this reason values become the glue for successful organizations, those that are able to generate sustainable returns in the long term for their shareholders and their stakeholders."*

In an article published on Harvard Business Review in 2002[16] Patrick Lencioni identifies four different types of values:

Core Values, which are the deeply ingrained principles that guide all of a company's actions; they serve as its cultural cornerstones. As such, they are the source of a company's distinctiveness and must be maintained at all costs.

Aspirational Values, which are those that a company needs to succeed in the future but currently lacks. A company may need to develop a new value to support a new strategy, for example, or to meet the requirements of a changing market or industry.

Permission-to-play values, which simply reflect the minimum behavioral and social standards required of any employee. They tend not to vary much across companies and as such are not really distinctive unless they are upheld with particularly high standards, in which case they may actually be viewed as core values.

Accidental values, which arise spontaneously without being cultivated and take hold over time. They usually reflect the common interests or personalities of the organization's employees. Accidental values can be good for a company, such as when they create an atmosphere of inclusivity, but they can also be negative, as the Enron case has taught us.

---

16 "Make your values mean something" by Patrick M. Lencioni, *Harvard Business Review*, July 2002.

Although aspirational values may also represent an important driver for positive change, among the different types of values defined by Lencioni, it is the core values that deserve special attention, as they represent the essence of the company's identity.

Why bother creating a values-driven organization?

Values inform and influence behaviors and decisions. No matter how many procedures, rules, and decision-making processes an organization designs, there will always be myriad situations where employees face choices that cannot be properly regulated upfront.

In the absence of clear guidelines that can support the decision to be made, decisions are often driven by the specific goals of the decision maker, goals that do not necessarily serve a broader company purpose. As an example, an employee could make a decision driven by the goal of generating cost savings, which, without even fully realizing it, may in turn negatively impact on the relationship with a specific customer. If in this case one of the core values defined by and lived in the organization was "clients first", then perhaps the employee would have made a different decision driven by a more elevated principle.

Establishing clear core values that are embraced by employees can help to set the desired standards in areas that are particularly relevant for the business and to create social norms that individuals in the organization choose to commit to.

An article published by The Economist in 2011[17] mentions the case of WALMART. As the world's largest retailer WALMART realized that its rule-based culture, which was codifying how nearly every employee's action was supposed to be done, had become too inflexible to cope with the challenges of globalization and technological change. Since then, WALMART has been

---

17 "Corporate Culture – The view from the top, and the bottom," *The Economist*, September 2011.

implementing a "value-based" culture, in which employees can be trusted to do the right thing because they know what the firm stands for. As one may imagine, this change has led to a drastic simplification in processes and procedures, which has made the organization much more agile.

Philippe Barrois, former CEO of Novartis France, states that: "*The stronger the values, the less process you need.*"

Values help to attract and retain the right people. Another good reason why values should be carefully defined and implemented is that they can be used to attract and retain the "right" employees. It's becoming more and more obvious to organizations that hiring the persons who will best fit their teams is much more important than hiring someone based on his or her technical skills.

Way too often companies face the costly consequences of recruiting new employees based on their experience and expertise rather than on criteria that would better inform the level of fit between the candidate and their future working environment. The company values can determine if the potential new hire will be able to engage effectively with the future team and with the broader organization, thus limiting the dangers of clashes that may arise in the future between them.

In other words, if you want your company to be innovative, you'll need a team of curious, daring, and creative people. The best way to hire and keep such people is to already have an office filled with like-minded individuals who share the same values and make sure that when new hires are made these qualities are assessed as thoroughly as any other technical skill.

Zappos, the US on-line shoe and clothing shop that was acquired by Amazon in 2009, has become one of the most successful case histories of how a company can build a culture based on shared values that are lived by all employees and that represent one of the main forces behind the company's success. Today thousands of companies from around the world travel to the Las Vegas Headquarters to see how Zappos's employees live their 10 values.

Values represent a competitive advantage. Core values educate clients and potential customers about the company's purpose and clarify the identity of the company. Having a set of specific core values that speak to the customers and stakeholders is something that can create an emotional connection with them and differentiate the company from other competitors.

For example, if we take Whole Foods Market, one of America's leading supermarket chains, its core values include selling the highest quality natural and organic products and promoting healthy eating education. Although other shops may offer a selection of natural and organic items, customers who value an organic lifestyle, sustainable agriculture, and healthy eating are likely to use Whole Foods Market to meet their needs.

Another example of a company which holds true to its core beliefs is Starbucks. Their values include ethical sourcing, environmental stewardship, and community involvement. Customers who truly identify with these values are willing to pay a premium for their products as opposed to purchasing coffee from a less expensive vendor.

Values in AEquacy

Aequal organizations are values-driven organizations, where core values are defined by the associates as a way to represent the identity and philosophy of the company they work for. The process that leads to the identification of the core values must be participatory and has to be consistent with the organization's Guiding Principles.

It's also important that the chosen core values are inspired by and coherent with the company's higher purpose and shared by all. This means that core values are not pre-defined and should be distinctive of how a specific organization wants to be perceived internally as well as externally.

There is also another type of values embedded in AEquacy systems, which are called Supporting Values. Unlike the core values, these are pre-defined and must be present in all aequal organizations, since they represent the foundation upon which the principles of self-organization operate to create a healthy and productive working environment.

In our research project we spent a considerable amount of time studying which values would best fit the AEquacy environment, which is built around a network of self-organizing teams. In our reflections we drew from different sources of inspiration.

In twenty years of experience spent in the area of culture transformation we've had the chance to study which values characterize a healthy working environment and which values inhibit the potential of the organization. On various occasions the scope of these initiatives involved creating a culture that supports collaboration, empowerment, teamwork, and entrepreneurial spirit, to name a few. Our findings were pretty consistent and clearly showed what employees were seeking in order to be at their best.

We also analyzed the results of the survey by Barrett Values Centre that we briefly introduced in Chapter 1 of the book, which reports how employees see the ideal culture of the organization they work for and which clearly indicates certain values that keep recurring.

The other interesting consideration that emerged from this analysis is that whereas some values can stand on their own feet, others seem to need something else as a prerequisite in order to be able to exist and develop. This effectively means that some values can function as a foundation for other values, which may naturally develop only if and when the underlying value is in place.

At the end of our analysis we came up with a list of four particular values that for us are best suited to the AEquacy environment and that also serve as underlying values. The four Supporting Values in AEquacy are: Trust, Accountability, Partnership, and Continuous Learning.

Although we are aware of the dangers that injecting pre-defined values into an organizational system may yield – a practice that we normally discourage – there are strong reasons why we believe that these four values should actually be a core element of AEquacy and, ideally, of any organizational operating system in general. And, to be fair, many of today's organizations are trying hard to implement these values, although often with poor results.

In AEquacy, however, these values tend to emerge as a consequence of many other elements that are naturally present in the aequal environment. The Enabling Context, which we explored in Chapter 2 of the book, and the Smart Systems, which we are going to cover in Chapter 4 create specific conditions that become a fertile ground for growing and nourishing the four values of Trust, Partnership, Accountability, and Continuous Learning.

At the same time, these values fuel and strengthen the elements of the Enabling Context, namely Self-Managing Teams, Peer Based Coordination, Distributed Authority, and Extended Financial Responsibility, as well as the four elements of Smart Systems, namely Information Free Flow, Radical Simplicity, Peer Feedback Loops, and Consent-Based Decision Making.

Thus, for example, trust may start to naturally emerge in a context where decision-making power is distributed or all information can be accessed and used by everybody. At the same time this implies that Associates who have to trust their peers will make the most appropriate decisions and use the information base as a source for value creation.

Does this mean that in AEquacy these four values automatically become part of the culture? Not necessarily; however, in aequal organizations there is a much higher chance that this will happen than in a hierarchy-based context.

Before delving into a more detailed definition of the four Supporting Values, we must emphasize a key distinction between these and the core values, which were discussed at the beginning of this section. The former do not represent distinctive elements of the organization, but rather a fundamental component of its aequal operating system. As such they support and discipline the ways in which the different parties interact with one another in the

AEquacy environment. The latter represent the identity of the company and its philosophy and as such they are a distinctive element of the organization and define how the organization is perceived internally and externally.

Both Supporting Values and Core Values represent shared and accepted principles that guide their associates' behaviors and support decision-making.

Trust

"The best way to find out if you can trust somebody is to trust them." – Ernest Hemingway

In 2017 the Edelman Trust Barometer annual global study[18] found that two thirds of the countries surveyed are identified as "distrusters" (which means less than 50% of the population trusts in the mainstream institutions of business, government, media, and NGOs to do what is right). This represents an unprecedentedly low score since Edelman began carrying out this yearly survey.

The negative results have been primarily fuelled by the shared belief of 85% of respondents that the system they belong to is no longer working for them. Interestingly, in the same study we read that the traditional vertical distribution of authority and power has proved dysfunctional across the different domains analyzed. The conclusions of this study clearly point to the need to devise new and more effective operating models for public as well as business institutions, based on a flatter and more participative approach, to re-establish the trust that has been lost.

If we look more specifically at the business sector, the situation is pretty worrying. In the article "Why don't employees trust their bosses?", published on April 2016 on the World Economic Forum website, we find some interesting and more in-depth information

---

18 Based on an annual online credibility and trust survey involving 28 countries and 33,000 respondents, carried out by Edelman Intelligence.

drawn from the 2016 Edelman survey. In this article we read that when it comes to trust, peers and employees in general are more credible than CEOs and that trust decreases the higher one goes in the organization.

Furthermore, generally speaking there is a wide gap between areas employees flagged as important for building trust and the observed behaviors shown by their leaders. This concept is further explored in an article published on HBR in 2017[19] where the author highlights some of the most frequently recurring manager behaviors conducive to mistrust, such as acting at the edge of ethical boundaries, hiding information, taking credit for others' work, and extreme focus on rule enforcement (control), to name a few.

Stephen Covey and Douglas Conant maintain that trust is the fundamental element found in high-performing organizations.[20] Interestingly enough it seems that although this link is in the minds of most leaders, very few of them are actively engaged in building trust in their organizations.

The importance of trust is corroborated by many findings. On the Great Place To Work website's home page we read "At great workplaces, employees experience high levels of trust, pride and camaraderie. The best workplaces go even farther to ensure all employees, no matter who they are or what they do for the organization, experience a high-trust culture."

In its March 2015 Research report, "Does Company Culture Pay Off? Analyzing Stock Performance of Best Places to Work Companies", Glassdoor[21] examined the stock performance for these companies over five years, and found out that they all have consistently outperformed the S&P500, up to a total return of

---

19 "If Employees Don't Trust You, It's Up to You to Fix It," by Sue Bingham, *Harvard Business Review*, January 2017.

20 "The Connection Between Employee Trust and Financial Performance," by Stephen M. R. Covey and Douglas R. Conant, *Harvard Business Review*, July 2016.

21 Glassdoor Economic Research shares insights and conducts research on today's labor market. www.glassdoor.com.

243% (versus 121% for the S&P500 during the same time).[22]

Coming back to Covey and Conant, their article cited above also highlights the link between trust and business results, through the impact trust generates on speed and costs: when trust goes down, speed goes down and costs go up, and vice versa.

A global survey commissioned by EY from Harris Poll in 2016[23] linked trust to other key metrics for business success, such as employee engagement, productivity, and ability to innovate. The survey also reported that the lack of trust in the surveyed cases was mainly driven by "unfair employee compensation, unequal opportunity for pay and promotion, lack of leadership, high employee turnover and a work environment not conducive to collaboration."

We are now clear about the importance of trust and what causes the lack of it. But what is trust really? And what about the factors that promote trust in the workplace?

Wikipedia explains trust by referring to a situation where "*One party (trustor) is willing to rely on the actions of another party (trustee). In addition, the trustor (voluntarily or forcedly) abandons control over the actions performed by the trustee. As a consequence, the trustor is uncertain about the outcome of the other's actions; they can only develop and evaluate expectations. The uncertainty involves the risk of failure or harm to the trustor if the trustee will not behave as desired.*"

Therefore, according to this definition, trust exists so long as the person who places trust onto someone else is willing to let go of control over that someone's actions. On this basis it should be quite obvious why in hierarchical organizations, whose culture is heavily based on control mechanisms, fostering trust remains a challenge often undealt with. In other words, a control-based

---

22 S&P500 is the abbreviated version of Standard & Poor's 500, an American stock market index based on the market capitalizations of 500 large companies having common stock listed on the NYSE or NASDAQ.

23 "Global Generation Survey," conducted by Harris Poll on behalf of EY in 2016 with nearly 10,000 adults surveyed in 8 countries on different continents.

culture inhibits the creation of trust.

Another interesting angle from which to approach the issue is to look at the most frequently recurring mindsets that most employees normally have with regard to trust.

Very often in our workshops with our clients we explore what trust means for them and how they can develop relationships based on a deeper sense of trust. One of the questions that we tend to ask early on in these conversations is how long it usually takes for them to build trust. Most of those who are asked the question tend to reply by saying that building trust takes a long time; people need to prove again and again that they are trustworthy before trust can be given to them. In other words, trust is given based on preset conditions that are important for us and that define who deserves our trust. We call this conditional trust.

As Charles Feltman writes in The Thin Book of Trust: "*having someone's limited and conditional trust is ok in some circumstances, but means you have to negotiate each transaction. (...) Such limited, conditional trust does not serve people who need to work together effectively for their mutual success.*"

In the business world, some of the possible consequences of conditional trust are well known: micromanagement, control, demotivation, disempowerment, stress, decreased self-confidence, lack of creativity, the struggle to fully express one's own potential, to name a few. We constantly encounter these issues in our work and we all know how damaging they can all be for leaders, teams, and organizations.

Furthermore, the notion that trust can be interpreted as a purely rational process based on the evaluation of others' actions and behaviors has been challenged by recent research in neuroscience and psychology. For instance, the neuroscientist John Coates proved that when we calculate and project future risks, including when we are evaluating whether someone is worth our trust, we do much more than merely think about it. Our body and the brain, expecting an action, start preparing for it physically. Willis and Todorov (2006) have shown that one hundred milliseconds of exposure to neutral faces is sufficient for people to make judgments of facial trustworthiness. This effectively means that trust is intrinsically biological and does not exist in the form of pure reason: that we thus have much less control than we think over our choice to trust or not trust others, since part of our trust-giving process is totally unconscious.

A 2009 study by Deloitte talks about the need and importance for organizations to shift their management style from control to trust.[24] The point they make is that the increasing complexity, uncertainty, and competition faced by organizations unconsciously generates a control mindset, whereby managers micro-manage all activities, do not take risks, and squeeze every person to the limit. This control mindset emerges as a futile attempt to preserve stability and predictability in a world that by definition is no longer compatible with these two concepts and that requires increasing levels of agility and flexibility. In its research, Deloitte maintains that the managers' ultimate goal – of making sure employees deliver the expected outcomes and do not abuse corporate resources and relationships to the detriment of the organization – cannot be achieved through control. Rather, it can only be achieved through an active engagement of all managers and employees in building and maintaining trust-based relationships.

The benefits of creating a company culture based on trust therefore touch many levels. The 2013 Cisco Collaboration Work Practice Study, which involved all employees at the global level, provides some food for thought:

- A trusting environment is a pre-requisite for developing innovative ideas, resolving conflicts with "win-win" solutions, delegating, and influencing.
- Trust has the ability to accelerate or destroy any business or organization: the lower the trust, the longer everything takes, the more everything costs, and the lower the loyalty on the part of everyone involved.

---

24 *Control vs. Trust: Mastering a Different Management Approach*, by John Hagel and John Seely Brown, Deloitte, 2009.

- Lack of trust significantly contributes to creating additional activities that do not create value, such as double-checking, bargaining, auditing of departments, politics, turf guarding, resistance to change, lack of collaboration, not listening, blaming games, and silo protection.
- An environment of trust functions as a releasing process; it allows people to focus their energy on creating rather than on defending.
- Trust promotes risk taking, courage, and innovation.
- Trust favors accountability.

AEquacy is built around the idea that self-governing systems are naturally conducive to higher trust among their members and that when people are held accountable and are empowered they are more open to building and nurturing trust with their peers.

In fact, the 2016 "How Report"[25] shows that organizations that are based on "self-governing" principles, such as those we have in AEquacy, present a percentage of trust of 75%, which is significantly higher compared to organizations that are based on a hierarchical structure, in which the perceived level of trust ranges from 20% to 2% depending on how strongly the vertical line of power is enforced. Interestingly in the same study, trust is considered a key enabler for risk-taking, generating 32 times more risk-taking, 11 times more innovation, and 6 times more performance compared to organizations with low trust cultures.

Jean-François Zobrist, CEO of FAVI, pioneered these concepts well before these findings were made. Strongly believing in the power of trust, he decided to drop control mechanisms over employees all at once. Most of the Management Team believed that there would be an inevitable and strong decrease in productivity; however, the opposite occurred and productivity actually increased. Not only that, but employees also declared that they felt much more accountable for their work and felt more

---

25 "How Report 2016," by LRN, based on data collected from 16,000 employees in 17 countries. http://howmetrics.lrn.com/.

responsible for doing their job well.

Before moving on to delve into the other three AEquacy Supporting Values, we want to make the point that trust can also be considered an underlying value, which is a value in the absence of which it can be hard to implement other values effectively. As Richard Barrett writes in his book The New Leadership Paradigm: "Trust is the glue that holds people together and the lubricant that allows energy and passion to flow. Trust increases the speed at which the group is able to accomplish tasks and takes the bureaucracy out of communication."

Accountability

"If you are building a culture where honest expectations are communicated and peer accountability is the norm, then the group will autonomously address poor performance and attitudes." – Henry Cloud

The need to increase personal and collective accountability in organizations has emerged more and more as a hot topic over the past few years. As a consequence, much energy has been spent trying to figure out ways to create the right conditions to achieve this goal.

In simple terms, being accountable means taking ownership and responsibility to complete the tasks or perform the duties required by one's role.

It should come as no surprise that, in line with this definition, one of the common assumptions underlying attempts to increase levels of accountability in the workplace is that accountability comes naturally when people know exactly what they are supposed to accomplish and understand the consequences of achieving or not achieving their goals.

In organizational life, however, objectives are often unclear and reward systems tend to lack transparency and fairness. Furthermore, the carrot-and-stick approach has proven to be far from what is needed to create accountability. In his book Carrots and Sticks Don't Work: Build a Culture of Employee Engagement with the Principles of Respect, Yale psychologist Paul Marciano makes a clear point analyzing how traditional systems of rewards and recognition fail to deliver on many levels.

To be fair, there are many other reasons why organizations today are struggling to hit their targets in terms of accountability levels.

Complexity. An increasing number of organizations are adopting some form of matrix structure, where the reporting relationships are represented as a grid combining the traditional vertical departments seen in functional structures with horizontal project teams, in an attempt to make more efficient use of resources, improve the coordination of products and services across departments, and facilitate the exchange of information. However, trying to nail down accountability levels in the midst of these structures can prove a very tough challenge, to the point that quite often it becomes virtually impossible to hold someone accountable for the end result that is produced. Furthermore, in matrix organizations it is very difficult for people to appreciate the true impact of their actions and contributions, given that many other parties are involved in the same workflow. In this context, accountability very often ends up being placed by employees "somewhere else" along the continuum of the workflow.

Fear. Generally speaking, accountability is perceived as something that happens to you when things go wrong, rather than something you own yourself to ensure results. This perception represents one of the main limits to one's willingness to take full responsibility for one's own actions and results, often resulting in cautious behaviors, blaming attitudes, and a lack of drive.

Flawed strategies. In hierarchical systems, strategies are normally defined at the top and pushed down the organization for implementation. This approach, based on the assumption that employees are unable to contribute to company strategies, has some evident drawbacks: it creates strategies that can prove disconnected from reality and, perhaps even more dramatically, it creates disengaged and disempowered employees who do not understand the reasons behind the strategies they are required to implement.

Management behaviors. These include the widespread inability of managers to establish clear goals and metrics and to have regular follow-ups with their people on the individual goals and metrics that have been agreed.

All this being said, what needs to be in place to create better conditions for accountability?

Make accountability a lived value

"When something goes wrong, the tendency is to look for the person to blame and, as a consequence, people develop shields to protect themselves. Other elements are the lack of trust, which eventually leads to more control, and the tolerance for dysfunctional behaviors that don't get addressed." Giglio Del Borgo, CEO Diners Club Italy, talking about derailers of organizational effectiveness.

Perhaps the most effective way to foster accountability is by making it an integral part of how individuals and teams normally operate. This means having conversations about it, aligning on what it means, sharing thoughts and ideas on how it can be nurtured, using it as an operating principle that guides one's own actions and interactions with others, and, very importantly, making sure that every single situation where a lack of accountability emerges is promptly and properly addressed. In a team or even a broader organizational context, it is about acknowledging that one's actions affect others' ability to accomplish their goals and realizing that the cumulative impact across an organization of one person failing to be accountable can be substantial.

Define the right goals and metrics and share them

If a lack of clarity of goals and metrics limits accountability levels, the contrary is also true: properly and clearly defined goals and metrics provide a clear idea for everyone of what's expected. This is particularly true in teams, given the dependency on each other's work and the exponential impact of not meeting expectations. When goals and metrics are shared, one's commitments become more transparent and this creates the possibility to develop mutual support. Moreover, as simplistic as it may sound, this also means limiting the number of goals to a few priorities that are simultaneously challenging, realistic, and relevant. Having too much on one's plate and losing focus of key priorities is a strong reason why people abandon accountability.

Make accountability everyone's responsibility

The complexity of today's organizations makes it impossible to define clear-cut allocation of responsibilities and it can easily happen that for the sake of effectiveness and agility individuals take responsibility and initiative where the responsibility is not clearly allocated. In the context of accountability, this means that every person in the organization should consider himself or herself as responsible for holding others accountable for whatever they are expected to accomplish.

Frame accountability as an opportunity to grow and develop, not as a reward or punishment practice

Accountability is about taking full responsibility for our actions and results, which in turn implies being willing to embrace the "good" and the "bad" that come with them. Often people avoid accountability as a self-defense mechanism, because they're worried about what might happen if things go wrong. In a context where mistakes are punished and people feel judged, accountability will tend to be pushed out. In contrast, in an environment where individuals are helped to recognize and value their positive contributions and see feedback on areas of improvement as an opportunity to grow and develop and, ultimately, become better at what they do, accountability is more likely to be taken on.

Build trust

Earlier on in this chapter we explored the value of trust, and there is a direct correlation between trust and accountability: in low-trust environments people tend to be more reactive and focus on blame, whereas in high-trust environments people tend to be more creative and focus on solutions. The first scenario is associated with lower levels of accountability and the second with higher levels of accountability.

Going back to AEquacy, we can clearly see how the whole model is built to support accountability. Trust and Continuous Learning are naturally integrated in the culture, Information Free-Flow creates the conditions for mutual support, Peer Feedback Loops provide the right context to celebrate success and address improvement areas, Radical Simplicity helps to keep the focus on what really matters, Distributed Authority creates empowerment, and Extended Financial Responsibility makes everyone responsible for the contributions and value generated for the organization. Furthermore, the whole notion of Individual and Team Mastery is about taking associates to a level of individual and collective awareness and effectiveness that transcends the fears and blockages that undermine one's determination to be accountable.

In AEquacy there is extreme clarity around how the overall organizational purpose relates to the team's purpose and OKRs and, ultimately, how the associates' purposes, objectives, and metrics relate to these other elements. In aequal systems, associates and teams realize they are held accountable, they understand what they are expected to do and they enjoy freedom in determining how to accomplish what they are expected to accomplish.

The Swedish company Spotify is a great example of a company that has applied many of these principles and that has managed to create high levels of accountability in its environment. Spotify is a music, video, and podcast streaming company with 30 million paying subscribers and about $3 billion in revenue. Its more than 2,000 employees are organized into agile teams, called squads, which are self-organizing and cross-functional. An article published by Harvard Business Review early in 2017[26] describes how Spotify achieves a balance between autonomy and accountability, and summarizes specific enablers for this: every team (squad in their language) has a specific purpose and each team is fully aware of its successes and failures. In these types of teams there is no formal leader; any leadership role is emergent and informal. On a regular basis, squads assess what is going well and what needs to improve based on feedback loops. Furthermore, Spotify employees may seek feedback from their colleagues as often as they wish, resulting in people taking strong ownership of their development and growth.

Partnership

"We will naturally pursue our goals on the strength of our own resources, skills and enterprise. But, we know that we will be more successful when we do this in partnership with the world."
Narendra Modi

The notion of partnership can be very broad and applied in several different contexts. In Chapter 1 we referred to the work of Barry Oshry and we summarized the conditions generated in hierarchical systems that may limit people's effectiveness and interactions. One important drawback of hierarchical organizations is that employees tend to ignore the conditions within which their bosses, peers, and subordinates operate and, therefore, why they behave the way they do in such conditions. So long as things work fine, of course, there is no issue; however, as soon as a perceived

---

26 "How Spotify Balances Employee Autonomy and Accountability," by Michael Mankins and Eric Garton, *Harvard Business Review*, February 2017.

lack of collaboration occurs, the most obvious reaction will be to blame others for not doing their job properly or for not supporting us as they should.

In Oshry's words: "Although we spend much of our lives in organizations and other social systems, we tend not to understand the system processes of which we are part. The costs of this systems blindness are misunderstandings and conflict within and across organizational lines, decreased motivation and initiative, the breakdown of promising partnerships, misplaced energy, poor customer service, and more." Oshry defines a partnership as "a relationship in which two parties are jointly committed to the success of whatever endeavor, process or project they are in."

Expanding this concept, the ability to build effective partnerships has a direct impact on the ability of the parties involved to deal with critical issues, manage a project successfully, and create an environment in which they feel more connected and engaged in what they do. However, building and maintaining strong partnerships is exactly like building and maintaining trust: it requires constant effort and attention. Furthermore, just like trust, a partnership may take some time to be built and only a moment to be destroyed.

All these concepts apply of course to relationships between people working in the same organization as well as to relationships with the different stakeholders operating within the larger system of any specific organization (e.g. customers, authorities, or suppliers).

Generally speaking, there are many factors influencing people's ability to build and maintain partnerships with others, both internally as well as externally. A very important one, as anticipated in the first part of this chapter, relates to the lack of awareness of the hidden dynamics that make people operate the way they do once they are immersed in specific working conditions.

The notion that the surrounding environment shapes our behavior is not new. Neuroscience demonstrated long ago that our brain is a meaning-making machine that constantly receives signals from the outside and interprets them based on our past experiences. Of course, the way our brain works is the result of thousands of years of evolution, and our ability to quickly make associations between what we see and past experiences is probably one of the most efficient survival-supporting systems that we have available.

Without it, simply put, we would not be able to cope with our daily circumstances. However, as effective and necessary as this process can be, it may also generate some very familiar unwanted consequences. The fact that we ultimately make up personalized stories of our experiences at any given moment, which is largely an unconscious process, quite often results in us making wrong assumptions of what is happening and making bad decisions based on such assumptions.

These very same mechanics are often the factors that, in an organizational context, cause people to express incorrect judgments about each other's behaviors and to blame each other and that, ultimately, create tensions in relationships instead of setting up conditions conducive to real partnerships.

Living the value of partnership

At Asterys the question of how to build and maintain strong and long-lasting partnerships with all our stakeholders is a very relevant one and we take it very seriously. In our experience there are several elements that contribute to building relationships as partnerships.

Holding a partnership mindset. This means considering those we enter into a relationship with as equals and holding both parties equally responsible for all the dynamics of the relationship. It also means holding fast to the belief that the quality of the outcome generated through our relationships with others largely depends on our ability to leverage our interdependence with them.

Mutual Respect. Respecting each other means valuing each other's ideas, considering each other a resourceful human being, and believing that better outcomes can be generated by working together and developing solutions and ideas based on collective insight, wisdom, and creativity.

Setting clear expectations. Engaging in a partnership means having a clear idea of how working together will generate the intended outcome. Setting and clarifying mutual expectations upfront is crucial to defining how to work together but also to determining what will move the relationship into a partnership space and keep it there, and what will move it out of it. It also means communicating one's own boundaries so that the other person will not have unrealistic expectations of how the relationship should function.

Embracing Diversity. Approaching a relationship with a spirit of partnership also means understanding that working on common objectives does not necessarily mean being aligned all the time. Being in a partnership means being willing to accept and welcome diverse people and opinions and to refrain from becoming judgmental or confrontational when interacting with others.

Trust. Trust is, of course, the glue of any healthy relationship and, as such, a fundamental element when it comes to building partnerships with others. Trusting each other is a powerful way to strengthen bonds with others and create an environment where both parties are more willing to align around a common agenda, to acknowledge their own roles in how they contribute to maintaining the spirit of the partnership, and to hold each other accountable for whatever joint result they need to generate through their relationship.

Sharing information. Communication happens all the time and through a variety of means. Effective communication also involves sharing any information that can enable others to be successful in their roles. Ultimately, a partnership also means being able to have open, honest communication and to refrain from hoarding information as a way to exercise power.

Taking responsibility for the relationship. This means realizing that as soon as we interact with others, whatever happens in the relationship is no longer the result of our isolated individual action but rather the consequence of more complex dynamics that emerge from the interaction itself. Since both parties contribute to the interaction one way or another, both parties contribute to the quality of the relationship through their own actions, behaviors, and responses to the other's actions and behaviors. Accepting our share of responsibility in the "partnership dance" is a way to invite the other to do the same and to keep a constructive focus on what needs to be achieved.

Sharing feedback. Feedback can be a powerful way to help others develop and it can also be one of the most effective ways to keep a partnership on track. Being willing and open to engage in conversations with those involved in the partnership on what does and doesn't work in the interactions is the best way to strengthen the relationship and block any derailer before it's too late.

Working on your personal mastery. Entering into a partnership is like starting a dance with someone else. Lack of self-awareness or system awareness often leads to an escalation of events that make the relationship fall out of step. Being aware of these mechanisms and developing the ability to own one's share of responsibility in the relationship is a key element to keeping the partnership alive and enabling it to evolve successfully.

Continuous learning

An article[27] published by McKinsey in September 2017 explains how the future of work will look as a consequence of technological disruptive trends, and what people in organizations will have to do in order to keep up. The key point is that for workers of the future the ability to adapt their skills to the changing needs of the workplace will be critical, which implies that environments characterized by continuous learning will be the norm. In the same

---

27 "Getting ready for the future of work." *McKinsey Quarterly*, September 2017.

article Robert Kegan, Professor of Adult Learning and Professional Development at Harvard Graduate School of Education, states that work will increasingly be about adaptive challenges, the ones that artificial intelligence and robots will be less good at meeting, and that therefore, there will be an increasing need for people with growth mindsets.

The distinction between growth mindsets and fixed mindsets was first introduced by Dr. Carol Dweck[28] to describe the underlying beliefs people have about learning and intelligence. A fixed mindset assumes that our character, intelligence, and creativity are static, and that success is the affirmation of that inherent intelligence. Under this paradigm, striving for success and avoiding failure at all costs becomes a way of maintaining the sense of being smart or skilled. A growth mindset, on the other hand, thrives on challenge and sees failure as an opportunity for growth and for stretching our existing abilities. These two mindsets seem to drive our behavior and our relationships with success and failure to a large extent in both professional and personal contexts. Research conducted by Dr. Dweck and her team showed that people educated on how the brain grows with learning show a strong increase in effort and motivation in their tasks and higher than average results in their endeavors. We believe that this is particularly important for at least two reasons. The first is that people who embrace continuous learning as a way of living their work and, more generally, their lives, have a better opportunity to succeed and generate value within the context of the future working environment. The second is that every person has embedded within him or herself the possibility to leverage or acquire a growth mindset to make this possible.

Although the complexity of today's business context makes this a hot topic, the importance of creating an organization with an environment conducive to the ongoing learning of its members, generally referred to as a "learning organization", flourished in the

---

28 *Mindset: The New Psychology of Success*, by Carol Dweck, 2007.

1990s, thanks to the work of Peter Senge. In his book The Fifth Discipline, Senge describes learning organizations as places *"where people continually expand their capacity to create the results they truly desire, where new and expansive patterns of thinking are nurtured, where collective aspiration is set free, and where people are continually learning how to learn together."*[29]

In order to make this possible, it's important to address both the context in which people operate and the mindset that drives their behaviors and choices in that specific context.

An article[30] published by Harvard Business Review in 2008 attempts to address the first of these elements, the context, by identifying specific building blocks that are necessary to foster a learning environment:

Psychological safety. This is the possibility for employees to be comfortable expressing their thoughts about their work without fear of being judged or punished when disagreeing with others.

Appreciation of differences and openness to new ideas. Recognizing the value of competing or diverse worldviews or ideas helps to increase energy, ignite fresh thinking, and prevent creative paralysis.

Time for reflection. When people are too busy with their tasks and activities or overstressed by deadlines, their ability to think analytically and creatively is compromised. They spend all their time "in the dance" and little or no time "on the balcony."[31] Supportive learning environments allow time for a pause in the action and time to take a more critical and conscious look at one's situation.

Concrete learning processes and practices. Learning processes involve the generation, collection, interpretation, and dissemination of information. For maximum impact, knowledge must be shared in systematic and clearly defined ways. Sharing

---

29 *The Fifth Discipline*, by Peter M. Senge, 1990.
30 "Is Yours a Learning Organization?" by David A. Garvin, Amy C. Edmondson, Francesca Gino, *Harvard Business Review*, March 2008.
31 As introduced in Chapter 1.

can take place among individuals, groups, or entire organizations and can be internally or externally oriented.

Leadership that reinforces learning. In a typical hierarchical structure, when leaders actively invest time to listen to, dialogue with, and debate with the employees, by so doing they are also creating the conditions for these employees to step into a learning mindset. In aequal organizations, where there are no leaders, this important role needs to be integrated by all associates.

As anticipated, having the right learning context is a key part of creating learning organizations but not the only one. Another important factor that contributes to how much people will eventually integrate the value of continuous learning relates to the type of mindsets they hold, which may in some cases facilitate and in others hinder their ability to leverage any learning opportunity that presents itself in the workplace.

In order to understand better what it means to have a mindset that favors continuous learning we need to take a small detour and explore in more detail what we mean by mindset. From a neurological perspective, our brain is constantly creating and destroying neural pathways, forming the thought and behavior patterns it uses to make decisions, choose actions, and present us to the outside world. The more a pathway is used, the stronger it gets. And the converse is also true: pathways that are used less tend to weaken over time. Our mental habits, or mindsets, are represented by specific pathways and our stronger mental habits unconsciously drive the way we interpret the world around us and, based on these interpretations, how we behave and the decisions we make. It's like always wearing lenses that define and color our experience of the world. A certain lens may suggest that volunteering for a new task or project at work could be a threatening experience, and therefore one to be avoided. A different lens may suggest, with reference to the same situation, that this could be a fantastic opportunity to learn something new. The problem with this is that, as the process is unconscious, we tend to forget that the lens we are wearing is just one of the possible lenses that are potentially available to us. And not necessarily the one that we need the most.

Luckily, the most recent studies in neuroplasticity prove that as hard-wired as neuropathways in our brains can be, there is always the possibility to create new pathways that serve us better.

If creating a continuous learning culture means making an organization more agile, more resilient, more creative, and even smarter, helping people to adopt a continuous learning mindset, or a growth mindset in Dr. Dweck's language, is the most effective way to put them in the best possible condition to be at their best.

There is a lot that organizations and their people can do to acquire or strengthen a continuous learning mindset.

Teaching about mindsets. Studies show that the mere exposure to specific concepts initiates the formation of new neural pathways. Sharing knowledge on how our brain works, what drives our behaviors, and how every person has the possibility to upgrade the way he/she operates in the world can prove a first important step towards raising awareness and starting the collective mindset shift.

Developing the ability to shift one's mindset. As we will see in Chapter 5, the work to develop Personal Mastery can prove extremely useful not only for becoming more aware of the origin of our mindsets, but also for developing the ability to replace limiting mindsets with new ones that serve us better. With reference to continuous learning, this means firmly embracing the belief that talents and skills can be honed by applying oneself.

Accepting imperfections. Human beings are not perfect, by definition. When people feel judged for their weaknesses they tend to hide them, which prevents a conscious effort to overcome them. In contrast, when people feel part of an environment focused on self-improvement, they will be more open to accepting their imperfections and to working on their development.

Viewing failure as a learning opportunity. It may seem obvious, but the reality is that most people judge themselves and are afraid of others' judgments when confronted with failure. Looking at failure as a learning opportunity requires not only a safe surrounding environment but also self-compassion and a willingness to apply extra effort to significantly improve one's own results.

Being a curious learner. A healthy baby at birth has about 100 billion neurons, nearly twice as many neurons as adults, in a brain that's half the size. This massive number of neurons is necessary for the tremendous amount of learning a baby has to do in its first year of life. Although it is not possible to reproduce the biological conditions of that period of our lives, living life in wonderment and discovery as a child would do, asking questions driven by an authentic sense of curiosity, is a very effective way to continually focus on learning and growing.

Valuing process over end result. We all agree that the results we generate are important when it comes to creating a learning environment; however, a focus on the process that leads to a specific outcome is even more important. This also reinforces the notion that everyone is on a path of ongoing development, regardless of the specific results that are produced.

Asking for feedback and acting on it. In various parts of this book we touch on feedback and feedforward. One of the most effective ways to increase our awareness of our areas of development and to engage on a path of ongoing growth and evolution is through the external input that we receive from others. Of course not all feedback we receive is relevant, and not all is given in the most effective way, but keeping an open mind to the possibility that through feedback we can dramatically accelerate our path of development will allow us to leverage any learning opportunity created by others through their feedback to us.

Adopting a prototyping attitude. Sometimes one of the most dangerous obstacles to our learning is our desire to do the "perfect thing", as if the perfect thing really existed. The emotional investment that comes with this is very often so important that if what we eventually produce is not in line with the expectations of ourselves or of others, the disappointment we feel will likely prevent us from appreciating the learning that may come with it. Accepting the notion that perfection per se does not exist, we can much more effectively generate a better outcome by testing our preliminary ideas, thereby understanding how they can be improved, and by looking at these learning cycles as an opportunity to achieve the best possible outcome. Such an approach is a much better way to integrate a continuous learning mindset.

The Chapter in a nutshell

- Most often a company's culture and values are not addressed properly, leading to a toxic and inefficient environment, disengaged people, and high levels of stress. Companies that invest in their culture and live their values create better places to work and better conditions for their bottom line.

- Whether or not we want them to, values lived in the organization influence behaviors and decisions. Establishing clear core values that are embraced by employees can help to set the expected standards in areas that are particularly relevant for the business and create social norms that individuals in the organization choose to commit to.

- Values can also be used as a powerful filter to recruit people who have a higher chance of fitting into the new environment and team and provide a differentiating element that strengthens the connection between the organization and the key stakeholders.

- Aequal organizations are values-driven organizations, where core values are defined by the associates as a way to represent the identity and philosophy of the company they work for. Furthermore, aequal systems integrate certain additional Supporting Values, which represent the foundation upon which the principles of self-organization operate to create a healthy and productive working environment. These are Trust, Accountability, Partnership, and Continuous Learning.

- Trust is a key factor for organizational success. It is the glue that allows relationships to flourish, creating a stronger foundation for employees' engagement, productivity, and ability to innovate – ultimately proving a key driver in business success. A culture based on trust also allows a shift from control and bureaucracy to speed and agility.

- Being accountable means taking ownership and responsibility for completing the tasks or performing the duties required by one's role. Accountability can be supported by clearly defining what is expected from a specific role, establishing the goals and metrics to be accomplished, and creating an environment where the fear of making mistakes is replaced by trust and a shared sense of responsibility for achieving a common purpose.

- Entering into a relationship with a partnership spirit means creating a joint commitment to the success of whatever goals the parties involved aim to achieve together. Real partnership happens when those involved in the relationship hold a "partnership mindset", develop mutual respect, set clear expectations and boundaries, are able to embrace diversity, trust each other, and share information and feedback.

- A culture that integrates continuous learning as a value is the culture of a learning organization. This happens when the organization has created a safe context for people to learn from their mistakes or failures and are encouraged to take the time that is needed to learn from their experiences. Holding, or shifting to, a growth mindset, defined as the belief that one's abilities can always be developed through work and dedication, represents the pre-condition for living the value of continuous learning.

4 - SMART SYSTEMS

From Complicatedness to Simplicity

Yves Morieux and Peter Tollman, Senior Partners and Managing Directors of respectively the Washington and the Boston office of Boston Consulting Group (BCG), in their book Smart Simplicity make a distinction between complexity and complicatedness.

Complexity stems from the increasing, changing, and often conflicting needs of the different stakeholders and evolving conditions of markets and technology. Complicatedness refers to the mushrooming of organizational mechanisms (systems, processes, procedures, rules, and regulations) that companies adopt in an effort to dominate and control these. The more systems a company introduces, the less it will be able to take advantage of complexity to create added value and innovate.

In order to understand the increased level of complicatedness of companies, the BCG Institute for Organization created an index to measure the number of procedures, structures, and evaluation and approval processes that organizations adopted in the fifteen years between 1998 and 2014. This index increased by 6.7 percent each year during that period. If we extrapolate a similar increase over a longer period of 50 years, this would imply that complicatedness increased by a factor of 35 times in the second half of the 20th century.

Moreover, a big component of complexity is the expansion of the performance objectives employees are expected to achieve, as well as their often conflicting nature. The BCG Institute for Organization, directed by Yves Morieux, has measured the number of performance objectives in a sample of US and European companies from 1955 to 2010. In 1955 there were on average four to seven performance objectives, while in 2010 the numbers ranged from twenty-five to forty. Moreover while in 1955 none of the performance goals were conflicting, in 2010 from 15 to 50 percent of the goals were in conflict with one another. Managers and employees have a lot more on their plates today and fewer resources due to endless rounds of reorganizations and layoffs in the name of efficiency.

In the highly complicated companies in the BCG sample, managers spend more than 40 percent of their time writing reports and between 30 percent and 60 percent of their time in coordination meetings. A great part of the managers' time is completely wasted, dedicated to activities that do not add value for the customer. Work becomes disengaging and demotivating for people and produces waste, negative Returns on Investment (ROI), and tardiness in responding to the challenges of the environment and the needs of customers.

Organizations design and implement systems in order to try to move from uncertainty to certainty (which, in today's complex, ambiguous, and unpredictable environment is fairly impossible). Managers need both to feel a sense of control over operations, projects, and production, and to ensure reliability, repetitiveness, and reproducibility of outcomes. In principle there's nothing wrong with that, although accepting and dealing with one's own fear of not being in control is a much cheaper option than constraining the organization with unnecessary procedures.

One of the reasons for the development of complicated systems and processes is the fundamental distrust leaders feel toward people down their lines. Employees are considered unreliable, lazy, and irresponsible and so their work needs to be regulated by strict rules and regulations. Their behavior must comply with the expectations of their bosses and their performance assessed and incentivized with a very intricate Performance Management System.

Systems and processes ensure predictability of outcome because any activity is regulated so that work is done exactly in the same way. For some purposes this can work perfectly well, but when we consider problem-solving as a response to new adaptive challenges, the tested and reliable processes of the past will not produce the adaptive solution required. A new principle should be embraced: equifinality.

Equifinality emphasizes that the same end state may be achieved via many different paths or trajectories. In closed systems, a direct cause-and-effect relationship exists between the initial condition and the final state of the system: when a computer's "on" button is pushed, the system powers up. Living systems (such as biological and social systems), however, operate quite differently. The idea of equifinality suggests that similar results may be achieved with different initial conditions and in many different ways.[32]

Systems and processes in business

Systems define how an organization or a department will operate. A system is a core element that helps people run a business. We can say that the entire business is a system in itself, but within it, there are many other systems that regulate how the business operates. In our company Asterys, for example, there

---

[32] Definition by Wikipedia.

are a number of systems, such as:

- Developing new business
- Designing programs
- Delivering programs
- Marketing & Communication
- Accounting

Each system can include a number of subsystems. Following the same example, in Asterys' marketing system we have: speaking engagements, sponsorships, and online and social presence, just to mention a few.

A process is instead the sequence of tasks and activities that transform inputs into outputs and are needed to make any system run effectively. Processes ensure reliability, repetitiveness, and replicability of outcomes.

Usually systems and processes go hand in hand. While systems are generally stable, processes are subject to improvement and change.

We can make a distinction between work processes and behavioral processes.

Work processes are those linked chains of activities, often cross-departmental, that enable an organization to accomplish its goals. We can group these chains into two categories:

- processes linked to the design, production, and delivery of products and services to customers; and
- processes that are not linked to what a customer buys, but rather to information and plans necessary for teams to run the business – for example budgeting, planning, hiring, and assessing people's performance.

Even if these two kind of processes, let's call them respectively operational and support processes, are independent and unrelated, they must be aligned and complementary for a smooth business outcome. In traditional companies, these work processes are re-engineered regularly to ensure that they save costs, save time, and in general enhance overall performance.

Most existing work processes developed in the past, in response to certain conditions, or when the organization was growing and in need of more "structure" – sometimes with a very weak rationale, meaning that they have since become inefficient. Very often managers do not know why a process was created in the first place, and very often processes are not even created deliberately but simply result from managers complying with existing and unquestioned practices.

Behavioral processes focus on behavioral patterns. They describe characteristic ways of acting and interacting among members of the organization. They describe "how" a process is carried forward. In most cases, the behaviors stemming from a process are learned informally, in the course of socialization and during on-the-job practice, rather than through formal training programs. They can be deeply embedded and hard to change. The most important behavioral processes are decision-making, communication, and organizational learning.

To make sure the organization shifts to AEquacy in a sustainable way, we envision four principles that apply to the re-design of the organization's systems and processes: Radical Simplicity, Consent Decision-Making, Information Free Flow and Peer Feedback Loops. The first principle, Radical Simplicity, is intended as a guideline for re-designing the work systems and processes unique to any given organization, aspiring to make them leaner, more innovative, and more collaborative. The other three principles, Consent Decision-Making, Information Free Flow, and Peer Feedback Loops are building blocks of, respectively, decision-making, communication, and organizational learning processes that ensure the successful adoption of the AEquacy framework.

Radical Simplicity

"*I believe*" tells us Giglio Del Borgo, Managing Director of Diners Club Italy, "*that we always need to ask ourselves if the processes reflect the best way to serve our customers, because the two elements do not always go hand in hand. Sometimes people focus on creating a process to keep a risk under control without considering what the customer thinks, how it translates into a positive experience for them. When one worries uniquely about the control dimension, that's when bureaucracy is generated. And bureaucracy becomes an element that gets in the way of reaching a good final result."*

"All too often we are too concentrated on how to work and not on how customers would like to buy..." adds Hugh O'Byrne, former VP Global Sales Center Excellence, Digital Business Group at IBM Europe.

Top executives seem to be in agreement that processes do not always benefit the organization. More often than not, they slow things down, frustrate people, and lead to risk aversion. Everyone knows this, but processes keep proliferating. What we don't consider is that all too often processes stem from fear.

As one of the authors, Giovanna D'Alessio, shared in her previous book Personal Mastery: The Path to Transformative Leadership, there are 4 basic needs we humans come into this world equipped with, and these range along two axes: affiliation and control.

The two poles of the affiliation axis are represented by the need to be loved/to be accepted/to belong at one end and the need for

Image 5: The Fear Model.

self-expression/independence at the other end. The poles of the control axis are the need for safety and predictability at one end and the need for variety and unpredictability at the other. In order to feel complete and balanced, all of our needs must be met. If these needs are not met, then we develop a sense of fear. There are four fears connected with the possibility that these four needs remain unmet. They are respectively: fear of being alone/of separation versus fear of feeling suffocated by others on the two poles of the affiliation axis, and fear of the unknown/lack of control versus fear of boredom/feeling trapped on the two poles of the control axis.

The need to control is deeply ingrained in our being human, because over the centuries this focus has ensured our survival. The way that we, as humans, create safety and control is through predictability, and we can see how this manifests itself from birth when we look at newborns and toddlers. For example, they love to be told the same bedtime story over and over again. They immediately object when the parent diverges from the expected narrative. Kids strive for routines; any unpredictable change has an impact on their sense of safety and ability to cope with change.

Inside organizations today, we find a vast majority of people who have a particular inclination towards the need for safety/predictability – otherwise they would probably be more tempted by becoming a freelancer or an entrepreneur, with working conditions that require an orientation towards the opposing need for unpredictability and variety.

People who have a strong need for certainty and predictability love well-organized contexts, with clear and well-defined procedures. They want everything to be under control, optimized, and done in obedience to the rules. Their gifts are perfection, discipline, organizational skills, compliance, and reliability. Isn't this the portrait of many rank and file?

The growing uncertainty and complexity experienced today generate fear and favor a "control mindset": managers are more likely to concentrate control, to micro-manage, to rely on established procedures, to maintain everything by the book, to preserve stability and predictability. Unfortunately it doesn't work.

"An organization needs to have standard operating procedures (SOPs), especially in the pharma industry where companies are

heavily regulated, so SOPs in manufacturing, quality controls, clinical trials are essentials." Philippe Barrois, former CEO of Novartis France shares. *"But we also create internal processes that are not always needed. Sometimes, the more processes you set in place, the less people can understand what they do. Processes can be detrimental, they disempower individuals, and thus people check boxes but they are not fulfilling the organizational purpose."*

The forces at work in business today render control-based management approaches increasingly ineffective, but in the rush to codify and standardize any variable in any process, managers keep binding their employees' hands and feet with rules, policies, and procedures.

Every CEO is fully aware that the proliferation of systems and processes increases bureaucracy and hinders innovation, and many of them state that their top priority is to make the work simpler.

But they make the mistake of choosing incremental improvements instead of Radical Simplicity. As they remain obsessed by the need to control, the results are often poor. Moving a process from 55 steps to 50 steps is not a real gain; it is only a band-aid on a stab wound.

Our view of Radical Simplicity is to minimize bureaucracy and liberate people from all the tasks that are linked to predict-and-control: over-planning, reporting, seeking several layers of authorizations, and the like. In order to adopt Radical Simplicity, all people concerned with the organization, including investors and founders, need to shift their mindset from control to trust. We have learned about the component of trust in the previous Chapter. Here we just want to reiterate that when trust is developed in an organization, there is no need to suffocate people with rules and procedures.

Here we introduce some of the steps to creating Radical Simplicity:

1. Have a clearly articulated and shared higher purpose

When a company identifies a clear, comprehensible, higher purpose that is relevant for all its Associates, people connect with it, embed it, respect it, and fulfill it. It mobilizes people, it makes them proud to belong. With a purpose, it is much easier to align even hundreds or thousands of Associates with what the company stands for and what is out of scope; what is aligned with the purpose and what would be detrimental. Simply put, it helps people to discern what is right from what is wrong.

2. Establish a set of values

Clarifying the values that enhance the purpose and drive the Associates' behavior is fundamental and provides a real compass for decision-making.

"That's where the culture and values are important: the stronger the values, the less process you need. We are realizing that we cannot have a process for everything that can happen, especially in the field of ethics and compliance. That's why with a strong set of shared values you can help your people to make the right decisions in any circumstance." Philippe Barrois, former CEO of Novartis France.

3. Move the responsibility for the processes to the team level

When higher-ups are the ones creating or advocating a process, the focus is on control and predictability and the result is more bureaucracy. Moving the responsibility for creating the processes to the Operational Team level shifts the focus to what is best for the customer or the most desirable outcome. Operational teams are closest to the final customer and they have a good sense of what can or cannot be a positive result or a positive experience for the customer. They are also the first to experience the problems that may arise from the implementation of a bad process.

4. Implement the Radical Simplicity checklist

When designing or re-engineering a process, we suggest that before the team adopts a process, members share their opinions around five key questions:

☐ Does this process add value for our customers?

☐ Does this process make our work easier?

☐ Does this process make our work faster?

☐ Does this process represent the simplest way to accomplish the outcome we desire?

☐ Does the implementation of this process still leave people feeling empowered and trusted?

The team can add more questions to make the checklist more relevant for their work. Each team member, in the round, can share their answer (yes or no) and at least one example of how the process adds value, makes the work easier or faster, is the simplest way to accomplish what the team desires, and how it will make people feel. If there are two or more "NOs", then the team must elaborate a different solution for the challenge they are trying to address.

"*As soon as someone creates a process*" Emmanuel Mottrie, CEO of TMC International, told us, "*I want them to think ... do you need it? If you feel you don't really need it, don't do it.*"

As simple as that.

Consent Decision-Making

The way a team or a peer group makes decisions in an aequal organization is known as Consent Decision-Making. It was developed by a Dutch educator called Cornelis "Kees" Boeke right before WWII, when he was experimenting with Sociocracy as a way to adapt Quaker egalitarian principles to secular organizations.

The basic idea behind the consent is that decisions are made only when none of the members taking part in the discussion has a reasoned, substantial objection to that particular decision. There are advantages in using consent rather can consensus decision-making. With consensus the participants must all be "for" the decision. With consent they need only be not against. With consensus a veto blocks the decision and the veto proposer doesn't even need to justify or explain the veto. With consent decision-making, those opposing the decision must always have a valid argument for doing so.

With consensus, the common experience in organizations, both for-profit and non-profit, is that members voting against a resolution or proposal often leave the meeting feeling unheard and not considered, engendering a lack of ownership. After the decision is taken, it is very difficult for all team members to maintain a unified voice in support of the decision: the members who felt unheard will work against the decision, either at a conscious or an unconscious level, sending the rest of the organization a very confusing message.

Consent decision-making, on the other hand, leads to greater commitment by all members involved because they are all included in the process and are able to contribute information towards the course of action to be taken. Decisions are thus based on all available knowledge.

Consent decision-making is fast because the objections have to be paramount, meaning they have to be serious enough to prevent a person from supporting the aims of the group. And secondly, they have to be reasoned. A person has to express his or her objections clearly enough so that the rest of the group can understand and resolve them.

A typical consent decision-making process includes several steps:

1.   *Presentation*

The "owner" presents the idea or the proposal to solve a problem, and the driver behind it.

2.   *Clarification*

All members of the team have the opportunity to ask clarifying questions with the aim of developing a better understanding of the proposal presented. This is not a space for debating, offering opinions, or making objections: the only goal of this step is to better understand the proposal.

3.   *Reactions*

In this step, each participant of the team can share his or her reaction to the proposal. People can share freely whatever reaction they feel and there is no debate or discussion. The proposer can receive fresh comments that can contribute to refining the proposal.

4.   *Proposer's response*

After hearing all reactions, the proposer has the choice to amend his or her proposal and/or to clarify the intent. The proposer is the only one who can speak. The proposer can also decide to keep the proposal as it is.

5.   *Objections*

In this step, the coach checks if any member of the group has objections. If there are no objections, the proposal is adopted. If there are objections, they are first tested for validity and then are recorded without discussion. An objection is considered valid if a) it proves that the proposal generates a violation of the organizational purpose, values, existing policies, or any other agreement previously adopted by the organization; b) the proposal would hinder one of the roles or abilities of the team towards achieving its purpose; c) the proposal would create new issues; d) the objection is based on a well-grounded set of data and information. A final check on the validity of the proposal is the question "Is it safe enough to try, knowing that we can revisit it at any time?"

6.   Integration

If objections have been raised, in this step the coach guides a conversation that aims at integrating the objections, one at a time, by modifying and amending the proposal. When the objector and the proposer are both happy with the amended proposal, the coach moves to the next objection. Once all objections are integrated, the coach calls for another Objection round to make sure the revised proposal has no objections.

Consent decision-making doesn't need to be used in every situation. Teams, in particular when making operational decisions on projects, can go back to a simple majority vote if they can keep the process functional, while including and considering the voices of dissenting members. However, there are cases when consent is the best option for a team to evaluate issues and make decisions. This is especially true for decisions on governance.

Processing issues and drivers

An issue is any potentially limiting factor or situation or dynamic that can emerge:

-   At an individual level, as an emotional issue or perception of a gap between reality and expectation;
-   At an organizational level, as an individual or group perception of a gap between the current situation (or a situation that is anticipated) and the organizational purpose/principles/values.

A driver is what underlines an issue. If the issue is a symptom, the driver is the cause of the symptom. It is a description of what is happening that may support/accelerate or hinder/slow down the organization.

It is everyone's responsibility to reveal an issue and to allow a broader peer group to discuss it, as it may reveal a challenge or an opportunity for a team or for the organization.

There are normally three ways to process an issue.

- If the issue refers to a situation in the governance of a team (a problem with roles and/or accountability, with the policies of the team, with how the team functions), the issue should be processed in one of the periodical Governance Team Meetings;

- If the issue refers to a situation in the dynamics of two or more teams connected to the same Coordination Team (a problem with conflicting roles and/or accountability, with the policies of the group of teams, with how the teams collaborate), the issue should be processed in one of the periodical Governance Coordination Team Meetings;

- If the issue refers to an operational problem or obstacle related to a project, the issue should be processed by a peer group including the parties impacted by the problem and one or more members of the relative Coordination Team(s).

Information Free Flow

There are several forces that in the last few years have been advocating more transparency by large organizations.

One of these forces is represented by governments that, after the most recent financial crisis, want to ensure they provide the public with greater accountability. Another force is represented by entities that are able to make certain key pieces of information public, such as investigative journalists and NGOs like Transparency International, a global anti-corruption organization that regularly publishes the transparency ranking of a number of publicly listed companies, considering, among other factors, the clarity of their anti-corruption policy and their financial reporting. In the 2014 Transparency In Corporate Reporting report on 124 listed companies, 101 companies out of 124 score less than 5 out of 10 overall on a scale from 1 to 10, where 10 is the most transparent; 90 companies out of 124 fail to reveal any information about tax payment in foreign countries; and Amazon, Google, Apple, and IBM all fail to publish a full list of countries where their subsidiaries operate.

Lack of transparency may generate financial issues: many banks are reducing funding for opaque trading firms to avoid fines for sanctions violations.

Institutional shareholders and activists are demanding greater shareholder engagement to ensure more effective communication with the boards, and they are increasingly paying more attention to long-term value creation instead of just focusing on short-termism. At the heart of shareholder engagement, there are issues involving transparency, including equal treatment of shareholders in terms of quantity and quality of information released, or time-sensitive disclosure of non-public information. Thus, companies are encouraged to communicate more frequently and in greater detail with their shareholders.

Another very important force is represented by customers. The way to build customer loyalty is no longer linked merely with reward programs. The new, skeptical, and demanding consumer expects a company to develop a deeper level of trust, meaning to be transparent in business and thus to be accountable for its words and actions. Transparency in this sense affects culture, because it is about how a company is open about its operations, processes, policies, and strategies. Only when organizations build trust with their customers can they then create customer loyalty.

There are two elements in particular that help a customer to have a positive experience with a company. The first is knowing the reasons behind the key decisions the company makes – so that customers don't have to guess at its motives – and the second is having a way to provide the organization with input and feedback (that will be taken into consideration, of course). This not only increases the quality of the relationship between customers and organizations, but it opens up the possibility to involve customers in the innovation process. In a survey done by Microsoft, they found that 97% of consumers are likely to remain loyal to a company that implements their feedback. With a two-way, free exchange of information, customers have the experience of being part of the process and of holding the company accountable.

The most important force demanding transparency is that represented by employees. According to the American Psychological Association's 2014 Work and Well-Being Survey of more than of 1,562 US workers, nearly 1 in 4 workers say they don't trust their employer and only about half of them believe their employer is open and upfront with them.

Good communication in organizations positively impacts financial performance: companies with highly effective communication practices had 47% higher total returns to shareholders over five years (2004-2009) compared to those with less effective communication.[33]

Having good communication in place also helps to avoid the costs of misunderstandings. When we use the term "employee misunderstanding" we refer to actions or errors of omission by employees who misunderstood, misinterpreted, or were misinformed about company policies, business processes, job function, or a combination of the three. Back in 2008 the Independent Directors Council (IDC) commissioned a study to determine how much miscommunication cost companies on average each year. Employee assessment firm Cognisco conducted a series of telephone interviews with managers, HR and staff from 400 companies and found that companies with 100,000 employees were losing $62 million per year on average due to misunderstandings. At an average of $624 per employee, that type of loss can even impact smaller companies.

---

33 Towers Watson, *Capitalizing on Effective Communication*, 2009/2010 Communication ROI Study Report.

In the hierarchical organization, internal communication is often intended as a one-way, top-down process where a few leaders with knowledge of what's really going on in the organization cascade selected information down to employees through several lines of managers and supervisors.

We worked several years for an international pharmaceutical company that for the last few years had been setting up a yearly two-day offsite meeting for all its 100 top managers to create alignment on strategy and increase collaboration and motivation. Before we began supporting them to make the best out of this event, the typical setting was one in which people were grouped as a passive audience before a lectern and the agenda included several speeches from the CEO, the members of the leadership team, and generally a motivational speaker. All of them would speak at the audience with very little or no interaction. The Internal Communication Director in charge of the event was upset because, in her view, managers did not engage themselves, ask questions, or make comments after the speeches, even when invited to share their thoughts. How could they? Everything in the environment communicated to them that the only important input was that provided by top management, and the participation of anyone else was not really wanted or appreciated.

We insisted on moving the flow of communication from top-down to circular. Every manager at the meeting, in our view, could have something valuable to share. We transformed the setting from a theater-style venue to a U-shaped one and some of the sessions were meant to have people moving around. We suggested limiting the top-down speeches to a minimum and for each 15-minute speech we set up a 20-minute small group of participants for discussion and sharing. Suddenly participants started animated discussions in groups and provided input to the top managers (who were coached to listen to any comment and just take it in instead of justifying or reacting, so that people could feel safe to speak up). We introduced what we call "gallery walks" where participants would stop at different stations where other peers would share their insights and the status of key projects and where participants could provide their colleagues with feedback and suggestions.

We argued that people did not need to hear some guru from outside the company, however crazy, heroic, or funny he or she might be, to get motivated. On the contrary, the opportunity to collaborate and share freely would provide a higher motivational factor. The event, as we expected, was a huge success and it paved the way to breaking down the silos and to encouraging people to speak up.

The pharmaceutical company we worked for was not an exception. In the majority of the all-hands meetings or corporate off-sites we had the opportunity to attend – until we were granted the permission to revolutionize them – it was only the leadership who talked about the organization's overall achievements, current state of projects, upcoming new projects, employee achievements, and the like.

All too often information follows the flow of the organizational structure. A vertical, hierarchical structure, even when ostensibly flat, encourages vertical communication – hence the silos.

One of the key elements of the communication system within AEquacy is that information flows in all directions, and all information is available to all members of the organization. Because the work is carried out by groups of peers collaborating in the same team and in collaboration with other teams in order to express the purpose of the organization, every Associate is able to access any information, be it: (1) organizational – i.e. purpose and values of the organization, purpose of teams, roles and responsibilities of the Associates, existing policies, both at an organizational and team level, metrics and business results; or (2) operational – i.e. product or service development data, projects that other teams are working toward, emerging issues and how teams are addressing them, sales figures for a certain product or service, competitive analysis, marketing information and expenditures, etc. Having free access to all information enables

Associates and teams to make better and more informed decisions.

Technology is making it easier and easier to share information among Associates. There are plenty of online platforms that allow members of an organization to stay up-to-date on the life of the organization and on projects being run, or to access the web of roles and accountability and to collaborate more effectively. When information is shared freely in a circular way, everyone feels invited to contribute.

Sharing information freely contributes to building a culture of accountability. Every team is expected to share how work gets done, what policies the team adopts for good governance, and what the status is of the projects they are working on – all in a very transparent way.

To what extent can an organization be transparent with its members? The social sharing app Buffer, for example, shares all information about company performance, with progress reports on customer support, blog performance, business performance, and more. Not only does doing so increase accountability, it also highlights issues and encourages employees to find solutions.

Transparency is important at HubSpot, an inbound marketing and sales platform that helps companies attract visitors, convert leads, and close customers. It is at the top of HubSpot's Culture Code. Its internal wiki includes financials, board meeting decks, management meeting decks, "strategic" topics, HubSpot's traditions and stories – pretty much any data employees might need to stay informed and aligned with the company vision.

When members of an organization have a clear sense of its purpose, goals, and expected performance, they are generally more committed and motivated to contribute to the organizational success. They also develop a better sense of how their work can impact the overall performance, and this encourages each member to go the extra mile.

The availability of company information, especially financials, gives people a feeling of fairness and openness and increases trust among members, as well as between members and the organization. Every result can be benchmarked against available numbers.

A particularly sensitive piece of information to share is the members' salaries. In Payscale's 2017 Compensation Best Practices International Survey of 7,700 respondents, of which 5,136 were from the US, only 23% of the employees surveyed said their company had a transparent pay policy.

PayScale has developed "The Pay Transparency Spectrum" to help organizations identify and benchmark their level of transparency against other organizations. Level one is the least transparent; companies tell employees what and when they're paid. Level five is the most transparent – some call this radical transparency – where either everyone's pay, or the formula for all pay decisions, is shared openly with all employees, up to the executive level.

Transparency spectrum

"Here's what you get paid"	"Here's how we use market data to determine pay"	"Here's where your pay falls and where you can go"	"Here's why we pay like we do"	"Here's everything you want to know about everyone's pay"
What	How	Where	Why	Whoa!
1. Paycheck	2. Data Market study	3. Plan Strategy Pay ranges	4. Culture Manager training	5. Open salary Published ranges and salaries

Image 6: The Pay Transparency Spectrum by PayScale

Nearly half of organizations described their level of transparency as a level one (49 percent). At the other end, 6 percent of organizations claimed to be at level five transparency. The rest (43 percent) fell somewhere in the middle.

A separate PayScale study of 71,000 employees found that 82 percent of employees felt satisfied at their company even if they were underpaid, as long as they knew the reason why.

In an aequal organization, we suggest that each individual team discusses and agrees the pay level of its members, considering their skills and experience, their tenure, and their Profit & Loss, maintaining the salaries within a given range. When each team is accountable for defining the best and most fair salaries and they can compare their decisions with all the salaries in each area of the organization, it enhances accountability and trust, and it provides the opportunity to bring inequities to the surface to be discussed. Openness is the best strategy to ensure fairness and trust.

Peer Feedback Loops

In the last 10 years there has been a discussion among Human Resources professionals and Executives of large organizations in which the effectiveness of the current performance management methodology has been questioned. More and more companies are abandoning the idea of classic yearly performance appraisals and are replacing them with frequent, informal check-ins between manager and subordinate. Among the companies that have moved to this more dynamic approach are Adobe, Dell, Microsoft, IBM, Accenture, PwC, Deloitte, and General Electric.

The rite of Performance Appraisal takes away hundreds of thousands of hours of the managers' and employees' time. The worst aspect of Performance Appraisal is that it is linked to financial rewards and punishments, and this produces several drawbacks.

The focus of the appraisal is on past behavior, and as it takes place at a much later date than the observed behavior, it doesn't help much in supporting current performance or putting people in the best position to succeed in the future. It is an assessment process, not a development process. In the current context where markets, competition, and technology change continuously, employees need more up-to-date developmental input.

The traditional use of Performance Appraisals to allocate

rewards is no longer effective for many reasons.

- As Tim Hindle, a former editor of The Economist, writes in his book The Economist Guide to Management Ideas and Gurus, supervisors are now responsible for up to 20-25 subordinates (whereas in the 1960s a supervisor had an average of 6 subordinates). With so many direct reports, taking the time for a thorough review of each of them is an overwhelming job. As a consequence, supervisors often make appraisals superficially.
- Supervisors find it hard to have tough conversations about poor performance with their subordinates, so they generally avoid these conversations by being generous with average scores, unless the company employs a forced ranking.
- Finally, as a corporation flattens and reduce costs, there are fewer and fewer opportunities for financial rewards or promotions to higher positions, leaving the employees frustrated, as the Performance Appraisal no longer leads to advancement.
- The focus on individual accountability and on ranking creates internal competition instead of cooperation.

Furthermore, a lot of feedback is given from the point of view of the managers, who bring with them their history, their bias, their beliefs. In our work as Executive Coaches, we have heard many bosses wanting their direct reports to be coached on competences that reflected the boss's assumptions and not necessarily the developmental needs of their direct reports. For example, for some bosses we met, being tough and assertive was an important skill for their direct reports to develop. Toughness and assertiveness were not present in the company leadership model; these mostly seemed to be the personal preference of the boss. When this happens, people cannot own the developmental journey and they resist putting effort into achieving a competence they do not relate to.

In the current context, companies must rapidly respond to emerging needs and challenges; employees' focus and jobs may change several times a year; and team performance is much more critical than individual performance. This context requires a different focus on dynamics, on continuous development-focused feedback AND feedforward, as well as on both individual AND team development instead of just individual development.

Feedforward in the AEquacy system

Feedforward means giving someone future-oriented options or solutions instead of positive or negative feedback. For example:

Next time you make a presentation, I suggest that you stand straight, grounded on your legs, and make eye contact with the audience. Check if that generates increased attention and interest from the audience.

Or

For the next meeting, I advise you to share your comments and inputs on your colleagues' projects: your input is valuable even if you have objections and your colleagues will appreciate the opportunity for their ideas to be challenged so they can develop better solutions.

There are several advantages in using feedforward. It avoids positive or negative judgment and thus emotional reaction from the receiver, who will be more open to listening and embracing the input received; feedforward is solution-oriented and gives suggestions on how to solve a problem or to be more effective; it gives the receiver alternative options to experiment with; it focuses on what can be changed, the future, and not the past; it is inspiring instead of judgmental; it reinforces respect and trust between people; and it doesn't require lengthy personal experience with the receiver – even a perfect stranger can give valuable feedforward.

Feedforward can be offered any time a person wants to contribute to the growth and development of another colleague or a team.

Focus on team development

In the AEquacy system, teams are the most important elements of the organization: they are like mini-companies with their own P&L and their own governance. They make decisions about their policies, their goals, and their metrics. The belief is that a team is much more than the sum of a group of individuals; the team can perform at a superior level thanks to the diversity of viewpoints and competences of its members. In an organization where teamwork is a prerequisite for achieving innovation and creativity, team performance must thus be given precedence over individual performance.

On the one hand, it's the team that provides itself with feedback and feedforward, for example by including a session at the end of any meeting. It doesn't need to be a long session – even one statement or 30 seconds for each team member is fine, as long as it becomes a healthy habit.

At the same time, in order to take into consideration how an external observer perceives the behaviors and results of a team, the Rep-Link can ask their Coordination team or another collaborating team to provide them with some useful feedback and feedforward.

Seeking feedback from peers and coaches

In the AEquacy system, as we keep repeating, there are no superiors and subordinates. The structure allows for equality. This doesn't mean that the differences in skills, expertise, contribution, or qualities are set to zero and not valued. It simply means that anyone in the organization has the same rights and can contribute to decisions affecting their work.

One of the challenges in this type of organization is the potential lack of direction or input in the daily activities for moving projects forward, and the lack of performance feedback, in order to adjust one's own behavior or competence and grow. In traditional hierarchical companies, such feedback is given by the direct manager or the management, who have a direct, vested interest in their subordinate and his or her work. However, the boss may have a hidden agenda; for example, he or she might be worried that the subordinate aspires to leave the team, or management might want a certain project to be carried forward in a way that makes themselves comfortable. Their feedback will be influenced by the supervisor's needs and fears.

In the AEquacy system, the feedback can come from any peer and from any place in the organization, and it can be spontaneous or requested.

An example of spontaneous feedback is when, at the end of a coordination meeting, a person in one team wants to share some positive remarks or a piece of feedforward to another person concerning how they performed at the meeting. A requested feedback is when one person reaches out to one or more colleagues from their team of from another team, to get some input on a project or a proposal they want to put forward in their team.

Another good way to commit to regular peer feedback is by inviting Associates to pair up with a "buddy" and invest 15 minutes each week to give each other feedback on their most recent challenges and accomplishments. In some companies, this practice is already giving very good results. In Next Jump, an e-commerce company handling loyalty programs for Dell, AARP, Intel, and Hilton Hotel, a Weekly Meeting with two pairs of buddies and a coach has been established to facilitate feedback conversations.

In the AEquacy system, peers, individually or as an advisory board, are responsible for helping to provide their colleagues with opportunities for learning and developing. As we learned in Chapter Two, Coaches are available throughout the organization to support people, and one of their roles is to provide them with input and feedforward.

As the approach to both work and self-development in an aequal organization is continuous learning, the easiest way for a person to check how are they perceived in terms of their personal effectiveness is to generate reiterative peer feedback loops so that the person can make continuous adjustments to their route to success and satisfaction.

When peer feedback is introduced and performed on a regular basis and when all Associates are trained to provide effective feedback and feedforward, there are a number of advantages:

- Feedback is free from conflicts of interest, from colleagues who have a lot in common with the receiver;
- It's a way to connect and to understand more about each other's challenges and successes, creating a stronger sense of belonging;
- It increases trust among Associates;
- It inspires Associates to take ownership of developing others as part of their job;
- It inspires fresh ideas and suggestions for continuous improvement;
- It creates more openness, transparency, and candid conversations.

Technology in service of open feedback

We envision for any aequal organization a feedback and feedforward online platform where anyone in the organization can leave input and suggestions for anyone else. As we mentioned earlier in this Chapter, transparency and the accessibility of data and information must be part of the practices of the company, including people's and team's reviews.

It may seem scary to allow anyone to share their feedback openly. In a hierarchical organization this would be used by some with ill intentions to put some people down and reinforce the giver's own power in the pyramid. In the traditional organization, the success of one person generally comes at the expense of someone else's failure. A typical example is the internal competition to be promoted to a certain position: only one will get the job and all the other candidates will lose.

In the AEquacy system, given the absence of subordination and thus of internal power games and competition, feedback is given with the intention to contribute to someone's personal and professional growth, and this intention is reciprocal. Having all feedback in the open requires all feedback givers to be careful in crafting their input, so that it is clearly developmental and not judgmental.

We would suggest using the online platform for:

Regular peer check-ins – we envision a short text box where Associates can quickly share one or two feedback items right after they have an experience of their peers (in meetings or working together in a project, or just in informal conversation). It can include a "thumbs up/down" checkbox, if some sort of gamification is considered aligned with the culture of the organization.

Short 360 surveys – we suggest brief surveys with relevant questions linked to the desired behaviors and skills for each particular role or area. We recommend keeping the survey to a maximum of 10 questions with a space for comments and keeping the time required to complete it to 5 minutes. This will encourage Associates to share feedback often. The survey can be ongoing, in order to get a pulse on what is working and what needs development at any time, or it can be scheduled every three months.

Skills recommendations – Another idea to make feedback alive and useful is to invite Associates to recommend the skills of their colleagues, like LinkedIn does. This can be particularly useful when an Associate applies for a new role: the team members in charge of assessing and recruiting for the role can have an idea of which skills the person has built over time.

The Chapter in a nutshell

- As a response to complexity, most organizations have developed complicatedness. The number of procedures, structures, performance evaluations, and approval processes that organizations have adopted in the last 15 years has mushroomed.

- The intention of the proliferation of systems and processes is to ensure control and predictability, but the consequences are costly. They increase bureaucracy and hinder performance, risk-taking, and innovation.

- Aequal organizations opt for **Radical Simplicity**: they fundamentally reduce the number of processes and make sure that those remaining are simplified to their core. In order to adopt Radical Simplicity, all members of the organization, especially investors and shareholders, need to shift their mindset from control to trust.

- A principle adopted by AEquacy to speed up decisions and make them more egalitarian is **Consent Decision-Making,** by which decisions can be adopted if there are no objections to them. Those opposing the decision must always have a valid argument for doing so. The constant application of consent decision-making in Governance and Operational meetings ensures that all members feel heard, that better decisions are made, and that the team reaches a higher post-decision alignment.

- **Information Free Flow** toward all organizational stakeholders is another principle of AEquacy. Transparency builds trust, consumer loyalty, accountability, and a sense of fairness.

- In an aequal organization, **Peer Feedback Loops** provide a constant exchange of feedback and feedforward among members. This ensures the Associates' ability to develop and adapt to changing conditions and challenges and the development of a continuous learning culture. Making all feedback public increases accountability and allows any performance or behavioral issue that arises to be addressed in a timely manner.

5 - PERSONAL AND TEAM MASTERY

There are some particular aspects stemming from the very nature of an aequal organization that require new abilities from associates in order for them to be successful: a) the associate's experience of expanded autonomy and authority without a control system requires greater self-awareness and self-management; b) tasks and responsibilities which were once the prerogative of managers are distributed under AEquacy to all team members; c) peer-based relationships call for a focus on partnership instead of leadership.

a) Expanded self-awareness and self-management

In an aequal organization, associates are empowered to be responsible for their functional activity, and their independence and autonomy are very broad. Defining goals and priorities, following through, and solving the problems along the way – all become a personal responsibility. Potential collaboration issues or conflicts cannot be allowed to escalate: there is no boss to bring them to; they need to be addressed directly by the interested parties.

Each person is accountable to the team he or she is a part of, and to the organization at large.

It's not easy for individuals and teams to fully take on this autonomy, especially if they have had the experience of working for a traditional hierarchical company. In such an environment, eluding responsibility by taking challenges or conflicts to the boss, or blaming others for problems and mistakes, are common practices. Furthermore, some people have a preference for being directed and managed by a supervisor. In an aequal environment, however, associates are instead expected to take full ownership of their behavior and performance, to be flexible in responding to change, and to develop an entrepreneurial, self-starter approach. These are all traits that need well-developed self-awareness and self-regulation as key elements, enabling people to understand and manage themselves and their emotions, impulses, inner resources, and abilities.

b) Distributed managerial tasks

In AEquacy, associates are part of a self-organizing team. This means that the team not only defines its strategy, priorities, and tasks, but must also seek out, acquire, and manage the resources it needs to be successful (people, budget, services) – which means that each team member must develop some managerial, financial, HR, or regulatory skills as needed. Last but not least, the team must be able to form, develop, and govern itself.

On the one hand there is a much larger context that a person is accountable for and in charge of; on the other hand, there is the aspect of building, maintaining, governing, and eventually dismantling the team, which is a shared responsibility among all team members.

This level of accountability requires a much broader knowledge and competence of team management from every single component of the company, and a much higher level of awareness of self, team dynamics, and the system as a whole.

c) From leadership to partnership

Leadership development has been the focus of Human Resources strategies for many decades, and hundreds of books have been published on the subject. Moving up the power ladder of rank-based organizations requires building the ability to lead others, to influence them to achieve the goals the leader has set for them, to motivate and empower others despite the intrinsically disempowering subordinate position they hold, and to support them to change when it's time to move the organization in a different direction, structure, or business model.

In AEquacy, no one leads or guides anyone. Team members have the ability and authority to make decisions and rapidly adapt to changing demands. The peer-based system of organization calls for relationships based on partnership. With this definition we don't mean the legal form of business in which two or more people pool money, skills, and resources, and share profit and loss.

What we mean is that the relationship is among equals and based on interdependency and collaboration to reach a mutual goal. In this kind of relationship, as we anticipated in Chapter 3 when exploring the Supporting Value of "Partnership", all parties are committed to the success of the common project, process, or achievement they are engaged in, and they hold each other accountable. This encompasses the conscious and deliberate efforts of an individual or group of individuals to improve the tasks they are engaged upon. Mutual accountability is a key component of the relationship and it occurs when every member resonates with the organizational purpose and acknowledges its overarching priority over the self-interest of a single associate or team.

A good partnership relationship at work involves being open and transparent in communication and believing that each person has equal worth, as do their ideas. It means going the extra mile to understand one another, sharing mutual expectations, sharing power and, most importantly, speaking up for the good of the team.

When reflecting on the qualities and skills that can make a network of associates into a high-performing aequal organization, there are four that seem essential to us. These are:

Personal Mastery: the ability to develop awareness of what drives one's own behavior, including deep-seated needs and fears, and the ability to manage one's own mental and emotional states to ensure a creative response to self, others, and circumstances.

System Awareness: the ability to develop a broader view of the team one belongs to and the organization as a whole, to sense internal and external emerging issues and opportunities, including those of customers, and to influence the system for the greater good of the organization.

Collaboration: the ability to engage in productive and creative conversations and to seek collective learning opportunities even during conflicts, in order to foster innovation through purpose- and value-driven actions.

Team Management: the ability to maintain healthy team governance, to engage in inclusive and timely decision-making, and to self-organize in order to achieve the best possible performance.

Of course, each organization will need to assess the additional types of skills required by their members in order to be successful in their environment, including technical skills or the ability to support a specific desired culture, and to include these in the list.

However, we strongly believe that the set of four competencies we have identified, which are important in every organization, are necessary and indispensable if we want to sustain a human-centered, hierarchy-free structure of self-organizing teams.

We do not of course expect that each associate show mastery of all the skills from the beginning. Skills can be developed. But there must be the potential in each associate to be open to learning them. When an organization is built from the start with the AEquacy infrastructure and all associates must be newly hired, choosing the right people for each role is a relatively straight-forward task: time-consuming, of course, and not immune to hiring mistakes, but simple.

If we consider the case of an existing medium or large traditional organization shifting to AEquacy, then the company already has a number of employees whose roles need to be shuffled, who need to shift to an "aequal mindset" and to develop new skills. These people may or may not be motivated to make this shift. In the end, adopting AEquacy is more than a change initiative: it is a revolutionary initiative. We will address the AEquacy implementation process in the following chapter, but for the moment we can anticipate that re-assigning the right people to the right roles can be challenging, especially when the decision cannot be imposed from the top down and given that quite likely a percentage of the employees of the former traditional company will not be ready to embrace the new demands and requirements of a hierarchy-free, peer-coordinated environment.

When hiring, all associates involved in the hiring process (generally the members of the team the new hire shall be assigned to and one or more members of a Coordinating Team and the Source Team) must assess if candidates possess at least the seeds of these skills or an attitude potentially conducive to acquiring them before making the final hiring decision, no matter how technically capable or experienced the candidates are.

The risks of not doing so are on both sides, as they impact the new hire's engagement and performance, as well as the team's performance. Let's imagine that a new associate is hired in the Marketing Team for the role of "Digital PR Specialist" and that she is very knowledgeable and capable in her role, but lacks the ability to own her own mistakes and has a strong preference for working independently. The new hire could become frustrated by the constructive feedback she may receive as part of regular peer feedback loops, and by the team's continuous invitations to consider ideas coming from other team members. As she denies her responsibilities when things go wrong, the team could feel frustrated and perceive her as not collaborative, untrustworthy, and arrogant.

Coming back to the essential four sets of competencies, let's dig deeper into the knowledge and practices to be developed.

Personal Mastery

Personal Mastery refers to the ability to be self-aware and mindful of the impact our patterns of thinking, feeling, and behaving have on the people and circumstances around us and on the results we generate.

Personal Mastery has two components. It involves Self-Awareness, meaning taking ownership for our thoughts, feelings, and behaviors and for the part we play in every event or relationship, so that we can contribute to maintaining healthy partnerships with others. And it also involves Self-Management, or the ability to manage ourselves, transforming limiting mindsets and behaviors when they no longer serve us, and to take the initiative to advance our contributions for the good of the team and the organization.

a) Self-Awareness

When the quality of peer interactions is key to good collaboration and outcomes in an organization, it is important to develop self-awareness, which is a better understanding of the drivers of our own behavior. To do this, the popular Iceberg Model provides us with some key insights. In this model, the part of us that is visible to others – and even to ourselves, unfortunately – is relatively small. The difference between the visible and the non-visible parts is important, because very often we expect others to be able to understand what we think or feel, as if they had a crystal ball. If we do not open up and make our thoughts and our emotions manifest, we leave the field open to assumptions (and these rarely turn out to be correct).

While our behaviors are visible (although subject to interpretation, and that depends on the observers, their mindsets and beliefs), less observable are the thoughts or emotions that underlie our behavior.

Below the water line, in the non-visible part, we first find thoughts and feelings. What we think and feel has a strong influence on our behavior. Let's just consider how our behavior is generally constructive when we are relaxed and happy and how it becomes rougher if we are upset and stressed out. On this subject, Stefano Petti has co-authored four interesting articles for Harvard Business Review that link good performance to the ability to manage our own inner landscape.[34]

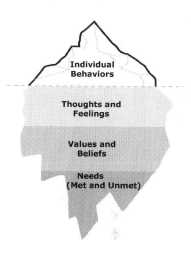

Image 6: The Iceberg Model

Developing awareness of our emotional states and being able to name the emotions we feel are the basic competences of emotional intelligence.

Underneath our thoughts and feelings there is another level where our values and our priorities reside. Our values are the drivers of our aspirations and intentions. They play an important role in our decision-making. In order to grow and develop, we need to be aware of our values and how these values influence

---

34 https://hbr.org/2014/12/how-your-state-of-mind-affects-your-performance; https://hbr.org/2015/04/4-steps-to-dispel-a-bad-mood; https://hbr.org/2015/06/get-in-the-right-state-of-mind-for-vacation; and https://hbr.org/2016/04/steps-to-take-if-youre-suffering-from-chronic-stress.

our decisions and actions. Our values may reflect what is important to us, what the culture we grew up in considered morally right, or our unmet needs. It is essential to be able to acknowledge that our values are learned, and that values represent a way to be socially accepted or may make up a component of a protective mechanism. When we accept this, we can shape our values, instead of being defined by them. This can be better understood if we consider the driver at the bottom of our iceberg: our needs (met and unmet).

From birth, in addition to the physiological needs of being fed and cared for in our basic functions, we have a range of psychological needs that must be met so that we can live and grow in a healthy way. As we mentioned in Chapter 4, these needs come in polarities:[35] one need is at one pole and the other at the opposite pole.

On the one hand there is the need for love and belonging: the child must feel the unconditional love of the parents or caretakers, as well as their recognition and acceptance. On the other hand there is the need for self-expression, to make autonomous choices as an independent being.

Another polarity of needs revolves around safety and control. The child must feel physically and psychologically safe. However, if the environment is always completely safe and predictable, it provides little stimulus to the child's growth and learning. So at the other pole there is the need for variety and unpredictability.

When at an early stage these needs are met – first by caretakers, and in subsequent years by teachers and classmates – then the development of the psyche has no limit. If instead these needs were denied or ridiculed during our socialization process, we may have been pushed to make trade-offs: concentrating on one need and suppressing another.

---

35 The idea of the polarities of needs in the iceberg model has been formulated our great friend, the coach Nadjeschda Taranzcewski.

We tend to adapt to the conditions of our upbringing and we each develop a center of gravity based on one or two deficiency needs. Deficiency needs are those that, when met, provide the person with no sense of lasting satisfaction but at the same time, when not met, would give a sense of anxiety. Deficiency needs drive behavior that is less than functional and that affects our performance and our relationships.

In any single circumstance, we can be driven by healthy needs that enhance our results, or by deficiency needs that hinder our relationships and performance. And we are too often unconscious of which need is behind the scenes of our actions.

The more we understand the origin and patterns of our needs, met and unmet, the more we can expand our repertoire of effective responses and behaviors. We develop choice instead of being trapped in autopilot mode.

If we shed light onto the drivers of our behaviors, we can realize that who we are is largely the product of our early responses to the environment and of our socialization process, and that we have the power to move from being defined by our drivers (needs, values, feelings, and thoughts) to shaping our drivers in order to unleash our potential and live a fulfilling professional and personal life.

In addition, the more we lower the water level of our iceberg, the more we can make ourselves known to ourselves and others and build trust around us, because we bring more of our thoughts, feelings, values, and needs into the open and in so doing we enhance mutual understanding. The other good outcome of lowering the waterline of our iceberg is that we empower others to do the same.

b) Self-Management

Self-management means that a person uses their knowledge of their own emotions to manage them in such a way as to generate positive interactions with others and motivate themselves in all situations. When we develop self-management we don't lose control of our own behavior, and our responses to circumstances do not depend on our mood or, even worse, on mistaking what is happening to us right here and right now for something that happened in the past and that once caused us hurt, anger, or fear.

Self-management does not mean that you can never become angry. There may be circumstances in which anger is a perfectly reasonable emotional response, but the key is to have control over it so that it can be channeled into resolving the problem at hand. There are several components of self-management.

Personal responsibility

When we develop self-awareness, we are more effectively able to self-manage, taking personal responsibility for our relationships and for our professional and personal life. This begins with a willingness to face any situation on the assumption that what we are, what we do, and what we have depends on us. This applies even to what is being done to us.

Personal responsibility does not mean taking the blame like a weight to carry on our shoulders. In fact, it is just the opposite: it empowers us. It means accepting that everything we create in life arises from our conscious or unconscious choices. Even when it seems that we don't choose, we have to acknowledge that this is also a choice. All that we are today, we have created. But by the same principle, we can change it, if we so choose.

Personal responsibility is not only a duty toward ourselves, but it is a "response-ability" – that is, the ability to respond to circumstances and events of life. When we take personal responsibility we are able to have greater effectiveness and mastery. First of all, we are more easily able to break the patterns of thought that prevent us from experiencing new opportunities. We feel encouraged to greater risk-taking by choosing the most appropriate and effective strategies. We can more openly recognize victim-driven habits of thought such as blame, denial, and justification. Personal responsibility also teaches us to use a new language for communicating with ourselves and with others, which includes being respectful, being open to others' points of view, and listening to understand.

When we adopt personal responsibility we become masters of self-management. We can look at situations through different eyes, identify what our role is, and know that if we are not experiencing what we want, we can do something different that will enable us to transform our thinking habits, behaviors, perceptions, and emotional responses.

Self-regulation

Self-regulation is one of the key components of self-management. Self-regulation starts with the ability to suspend judgment, to observe without the filters of our own iceberg. In a way we can say that we learn to listen and observe others in the most neutral way, so that assumptions, judgments, and beliefs don't get in the way of our understanding.

Developing self-regulation also means that we are not slaves to our destructive emotional reactions. According to neuroscientist Paul McLean there are three distinct areas of the brain that developed during the evolution of the human species: the reptilian brain, the limbic brain, and the neocortex. The reptilian brain controls all the automatic vital functions like breathing and heart rate. This part of the brain tends to be somewhat rigid and compulsive.

The limbic brain can record memories of behaviors that produced pleasant or unpleasant experiences, so it is responsible for what we call emotions. The neocortex is responsible for the development of language, abstract thinking, imagination, and consciousness. The neocortex is flexible and has endless learning skills.

Normally when we receive an input (a stimulus from the outside), the information from the eyes, skin, ears, or other sense organs is first directed toward the thalamus, a gland positioned in the limbic brain. Its function is to elaborate the information received from the sense organs and distribute it to other parts of the brain. In the thalamus, the input is compared to those that have been recorded throughout our entire life, to see if it resembles something we have already seen or experienced. If the information is associated with some "neutral" or pleasant memory, then the impulse is sent to the neocortex and we respond to our context in a creative and functional way.

When, on the other hand, the input received is recognized as equal or similar to a danger that we have experienced in the past, then the thalamus bypasses the neocortex – the "thinking" brain – and sends the information directly to the amygdala, an almond-shaped gland in the limbic brain.

The amygdala reacts according to the behavioral patterns developed in the past, by flooding our body with chemicals and hormones, such as adrenaline and cortisol, that prepare the body to react. Our reactive responses can be of three types – fight, flight, or freeze – so that we become aggressive, we withdraw, or we become totally blocked. Unless we are really in a situation where one of these automatic reactions can save our lives, probably none of these responses are functional, because they create friction and disconnection with other people and do not help to overcome problems or misunderstandings.

When we find ourselves in a prolonged reactive mood, we also experience severe stress. This automatic physiological mechanism of ours, called the "Amygdala Hijack," has been functional to our survival for millions of years. Even now, it is valid in many cases: for example, it is what allows us to snatch our finger away from a flame within a fraction of a second, before it can burn. Unfortunately it is also activated when it is not applicable to our social situations, whether at home, at work, or among friends.

Developing self-regulation means that we learn to create a space between stimulus and response so that we can train ourselves to access the creative power of the neo-cortex and dissipate the dysfunctional energy of the amygdala. Self-regulation helps us to be better observers and listeners and to respond to relationships and life circumstances with a broader range of creative behaviors, as well as being more effective during conflicts, crisis, and stressful situations.

Flexibility

Flexibility is the ability to be open to change and to adapt. In biology the term "adaptive pressure" defines a situation in which the effective response to the surrounding environment is not included in the possibilities and current capabilities of the organism. This means that the body must "observe" its processes and "discern" what still works and what needs to be abandoned – a process that requires a transformation, if the organism is to survive successfully in an environment that has changed. The same process should be undertaken by a person when contextual conditions change or when old strategies are no longer effective.

The challenges that we are often confronted with require flexibility. They require us to question the assumptions and beliefs underlying our way of seeing and interpreting ourselves, others, our circumstances, and the world, and to be able to reformulate them. We cannot expect to overcome today's adaptive challenges without profoundly transforming our mindset and our paradigms, without increasing our ability to maintain different perspectives and tolerate the contrasts between them, and without learning to be comfortable with uncertainty and the tension of opposites.

Self-starting

Self-starting includes self-motivation and the propensity to take ownership for and pursue goals with energy and persistence. In AEquacy, team members work autonomously and don't have a leader to assign them tasks. Each associate is expected to take initiative and build a great sense of ownership and commitment. Self-starters are excellent in sensing and taking advantage of opportunities, because their radar is always on. One of the qualities that self-starters show is self-confidence. Self-confident people usually possess a positive outlook, believe in their ability to make contributions, and are not afraid to make decisions.

When a person develops a self-starting attitude, their approach to work becomes thorough and careful. They are attentive to details and care about high-quality work. Moreover, they are focused to complete tasks and projects with the same energy and motivation they have when they begin.

System Awareness

In the last decade we have started to hear about "system perspectives" or "adopting systemic approaches" more and more often. But it is not always clear what is meant by that. One important distinction we have to make is between "systematic" and "systemic." Systematic is when I do something following specific rules, in a regular and methodical way. Systemic is when I take into account the larger context (the system or systems I am part of) and I consider the interactions and dynamics among the different parts of the system(s).

This perspective stems from the discipline of systems thinking or systems theory, which is dedicated to contemplating how systems work and how they can be influenced.

Contemporary ideas from systems theory have stemmed from diverse areas including ontology, philosophy of science, physics, computer science, biology, and engineering, as well as geography, sociology, political science, psychotherapy (within family systems therapy), and economics, among others. This demonstrates that systems theory is a transdisciplinary, interdisciplinary, and multi-perspective domain. The most important contributors who have impacted the business context are Peter Senge, Fritjof Capra, Francisco Varela, Humberto Maturana, and Ervin Laszlo, among others.

As Michael Goodman, an internationally recognized speaker, author, and practitioner in the field of systems thinking, describes:

"The discipline of systems thinking is more than just a collection of tools and methods – it's also an underlying philosophy. Many beginners are attracted to the tools, such as causal loop diagrams and management flight simulators, in hopes that these tools will help them deal with persistent business problems. But systems thinking is also a sensitivity to the circular nature of the world we live in; an awareness of the role of structure in creating the conditions we face; a recognition that there are powerful laws of systems operating that we are unaware of; a realization that there are consequences to our actions that we are oblivious to.

Systems thinking is also a diagnostic tool. As in the medical field, effective treatment follows thorough diagnosis. In this sense, systems thinking is a disciplined approach for examining problems more completely and accurately before acting. It allows us to ask better questions before jumping to conclusions.

Systems thinking often involves moving from observing events or data, to identifying patterns of behavior over time, to surfacing the underlying structures that drive those events and patterns. By understanding and changing structures that are not serving us well (including our mental models and perceptions), we can expand the choices available to us and create more satisfying, long-term solutions to chronic problems." [36]

Although there are different schools of thought and applications in systems theory, there are some elements that are common to all of them, as Bob Williams and Richard Hummelbrunner propose in their book Systems Concepts in Action: A Practitioner's Toolkit:

- Focus on interrelationships
- Inclusion of multiple perspectives
- Boundaries

---

36 https://thesystemsthinker.com/systems-thinking-what-why-when-where-and-how/.

Focus on interrelationships

Focus on interrelationships means that there is a strong emphasis on the connections between the elements of a system and on the consequences of these connections. Systems thinking is particularly concerned with some specific aspects of interrelationships, for example:

- The structure of the interrelationships within the situation (i.e. resources, employees, stakeholders, processes, information);
- The processes between the different elements of that structure;
- The nature of interrelationships (i.e. smooth, complicated, fast, slow, collaborative);
- The patterns emerging from the interrelationships at play, the consequences arising from them, and the people affected by the consequences.

System awareness is much more than identifying the different parts of a system and the way they interact with one another.

The second element, perspectives, can expand the concept.

Inclusion of multiple perspectives

System awareness has to do with how we look at the system. Thinking systemically includes how we look at the entire picture. When people observe the results of interrelationships, what they "see" is mediated and influenced by their mindset, their "iceberg". Let's remember that reality is only subjective; there is no one universal reality.

When looking at a system we need to consider not only the different stakeholders' interests, but also that each stakeholder group may have a different perspective, and even each single stakeholder may have a different perspective, which can conflict with those of the group of stakeholders he or she is part of. Developing system awareness means making ourselves open and sensitive to different perspectives and helps us to better understand the different system behaviors, and to have a deeper understanding of the behaviors that may seem, on the surface, to be merely unintended consequences. In fact, what we consider unintended consequences often result from our unwillingness to understand or explore other people's perceptions. Many times, someone, somewhere actually did intend the result that we consider problematic.

Moreover, if we consider different perspectives, comparing our views with the views held by people with different perspectives, we train ourselves to abandon the idea of the "one reality" of how the system works and allow ourselves to consider alternatives.

Boundaries

The other characteristic of system awareness is the acknowledgment that we will never be able to make sense of every element and dynamic of a system; we will never know everything about it. We then need to consciously set boundaries, to make choices of what to observe in a system, to decide which dynamics are to be included for the sake of the outcome we want and which are to be excluded – which perspectives we want to consider and which we want to leave in the background. The process of setting boundaries helps us to circumscribe what is relevant or irrelevant, what is important or not, who can benefit and who is disadvantaged, which projects are worth the team's time and which aren't. Boundaries help us to make the situation more manageable.

Thus, when we develop system awareness we navigate with the bigger picture in view. At a team level, we can connect potential issues we face with the inner dynamics of the team and not with team members' mistaken intentions. When confronted with a team, operational, or organizational issue, we don't address the symptoms, but we seek the root cause of the problem, knowing that the causes are probably inherent in the design of the system in which we operate, not in the people. Let's remember the predictable patterns of Tops/Middle/Bottoms/Customers in the hierarchical organization. Moving from hierarchy to a whole new paradigm of equality will surely bring to the surface new patterns of dynamics in the structure over the long run, and we need to be able to observe them and be ready to address them.

The more we develop system awareness, the larger our perspective becomes, allowing us to identify which changes, even small, in a specific place in the system will result in significant advantages for the performance of the team and the organization. We can see how the elements of the organization (production, supply management, technology, structure, culture, etc.) interact with each other and with the environment to produce outcomes. We can include our hypothesis of the impact of current actions in the way that we address opportunities and problems.

When we master system awareness then we will start to include a community, country, and even a global perspective, taking into consideration not only the health of our company, but also the impact it has on the long-term health of a larger context – and we can expand the (positive) impact we can have in the world.

System awareness in fact includes the network of relationships that the organization has with its economic, political, and natural environment and is dedicated to enhancing all these relationships to create win-win solutions: a win for the organization and for the larger system of which the organization is a part.

System awareness enables us to manage complexity more effectively, because we are able to see patterns and make sense of them in activities that normally present themselves as fragmented and bureaucratized. We learn to see the integration among all parts of the system, to simplify overly complex processes, and to redesign the system to solve multiple problems simultaneously.

According to James Ludema and Bernard Mohr, two of the leading experts on Appreciative Inquiry, *"...having the whole system in the room also brings an ecological perspective: all the pieces of the puzzle come together in one place and everyone can gain an appreciation for the whole. The unique perspective of each person, when combined with the perspectives of others, creates new possibilities for action, possibilities that previously lay dormant or undiscovered."* [37]

There are certain human qualities that support the development of system awareness. They are: inquiry, courage, and compassion.

Inquiry

Inquiry is a dynamic process by which we apply openness and curiosity to knowing and understanding the world. It is an attitude that colors all aspects of life. When we talk about inquiry, we refer to the process by which a group of people develops knowledge through working together and having conversations while they present and solve problems, and explore and test the discoveries that emerge from this activity. Inquiry involves serious engagement and investigation and the active creation and testing of new knowledge.

Curiosity is an essential ingredient of the inquirer's way of making discoveries. We are not used to asking exploratory questions, as we were not taught to do so at school and our culture does not particularly value curiosity. On the contrary, we have always been taught that questions have right or wrong answers and that we must ask questions to restrict the number of options, as the scientific method suggests.

Genuine curiosity is also able to strengthen our relationships with the people who are engaged with us in the inquiry process. When people are truly and profoundly curious, they awaken in others a sense of trust which enables them to reveal their

---

37 *The Appreciative Inquiry Summit: A Practitioner's Guide for Leading Large-Group Change, Berrett-Koehler Publishers,* 2003.

thoughts and become vulnerable, because the space that the relationship has constructed is a safe and judgment-free zone.

There are several tools and methodologies to help groups to use their collective intelligence to inquire into problems and issues systemically and come up with breakthrough ideas. Some of these are:

Appreciative Inquiry: Appreciative Inquiry was developed by David Cooperrider – the Fairmount Minerals Chair and Professor of Social Entrepreneurship at the Weatherhead School of Management at Case Western Reserve University – and Suresh Srivastva. Appreciative Inquiry is a methodology for collective inquiry that investigates the best of what is already there, then moves on to imagine what could be accomplished, and is followed by a collective design of a desired, and desirable, future state.

The methodology is based on the assumption that questions automatically influence the direction of the answer, and that organizations evolve in the direction of the questions people most persistently and passionately ask. The most popular methods of assessing and evaluating a problem or a situation, especially back in the 1980s and 1990s, were based on a deficiency model, where the focus is on what is wrong or what needs to be fixed or solved. In contrast, Appreciative Inquiry has moved the focus to what works, what is positive about the situation or problem, and what people value the most.

World Café: World Café is an easy-to-use method for creating a living network of collaborative dialogue around questions that matter in the service of real work. In a World Café session, small groups of 4 to 6 people discuss a topic around several tables for a certain amount of time and then participants switch tables before continuing to explore the topic. At the new table, they are introduced to the discussion that has just taken place by a "table host" and then they continue the exploration before switching tables again. There are generally three discussion rounds, and during the conversations participants are encouraged to write or doodle on the tablecloth so that when people change tables, they can see what previous members have written as well as hearing the table host's synthesis of what has been discussed.

Two underlying assumptions of World Café events are that people already have within them the wisdom and creativity to effectively address their most important challenges and opportunities; and that collective discussion can shift people's conceptions and encourage collective action.

The World Café originated at the home of Juanita Brown and David Isaacs in 1995.

Courage

In the average organizational setting, the approach most widely adopted to seeking solutions to problems is looking for "quick fixes" or seeking incremental betterment. The underlying fear relates to the reluctance to take risks in adopting solutions that are not easy to implement or whose consequences have not yet been tested. Such partial solutions can work in the short term, but often make the problem larger over time. Moreover, unfortunately, the adaptive challenges that organizations encounter today call for breakthrough solutions that have never been tried before. When we use system thinking to understand a problem or issue, we may generate alternatives that we would have never considered otherwise, and come up with ideas that may not be easy to implement or that may entail taking some risks. It takes courage to consider and take a stand for solutions designed for the long term.

Compassion

Compassion stems from the acknowledgment that we too, are part of the system and that there is no single part of the system that is to blame for the problems we face. When people reach this systemic awareness, they feel empowered to develop shared insights and alternatives that can solve these problems. As David

Peter Stroh[38] beautifully puts it:

"*Compassion points us away from blame and toward responsibility—it helps us see how we often self-inflict our problems, whether through individual thought processes or our group's policies and actions. The benefit of compassion and responsibility is power: the power to influence or accept that for which we have compassion and to control that for which we are directly responsible.*"

Collaboration

In the last 10 years, collaboration has been increasingly considered as one of the key drivers of organizational success. A confirmation came from the 2006 and subsequent 2009 "Meetings Around the World: The Impact of Collaboration on Business Performance" studies, conducted by Frost & Sullivan and sponsored by Verizon Business and Microsoft Corp and conducted on 946 managers from a cross section of 2,000 small-to-medium, midmarket, and global companies in the US, Europe, and Asia-Pacific. In the study findings, the three elements of a) collaboration; b) a company's strategic orientation; and c) market turbulence were identified as the three main business performance drivers. But collaboration was by far the most important factor: its impact revealed it to be twice as significant as a company's aggressiveness in pursuing new market opportunities (strategic orientation) and five times as significant as the external market environment (market turbulence).

In a 2012 IBM study based on face-to-face conversations with more than 1,700 chief executive officers in 64 countries, what emerged was that CEOs are keen to create more open and collaborative cultures, encouraging people to connect, learn from each other, and thrive in a world of rapid change. Being

---

38 David is the author of the new book *Systems Thinking for Social Change: A Practical Guide for Solving Complex Problems, Avoiding Unintended Consequences, and Achieving Lasting Results* (Chelsea Green, 2015).

collaborative is the number one trait that CEOs seek in their employees (75% agreement among survey participants), together with being communicative (67%), creative (61%), and flexible (61%). They acknowledge the importance of having employees who are able to constantly reinvent themselves, who are comfortable with change, and who can learn as they go, often from others' experiences.

A qualitative, ethnographic research study with Cisco employees globally, the 2013 Cisco Collaboration Work Practice Study, designed to collect insights into the human behavior of collaboration, showed that participants believed that the collective intelligence and diverse perspectives of people working together create better overall results. They described the experience of collaboration as rewarding, engaging, synergistic, and enjoyable. They also mentioned the frustration felt with regard to decision-making, which could make collaboration time-consuming, especially when a consensus could not be reached. Study participants mentioned the key elements necessary for collaboration to develop, which included: quality of interaction among people; channeling human interactions toward concrete results; an open and participatory environment that helps people engage with each other; and balancing decision-making with consensus-building.

The context, framework, and structure of AEquacy pave the way for collaboration. The presence of a strong organizational purpose and team purpose provides teams with direction and meaning; the absence of subordination makes people take more ownership and risks; and the importance placed on trust as one of the founding values of the organization makes people confident to express their opinions and ideas without worry of being judged, dismissed, or ridiculed. Transparency gives associates the feeling that all information is available and that it is good to share; the consent decision-making speeds up decisions while allowing everyone to be heard and considered; the presence of roles such as the Cross-Link, whose responsibility is to share information and cross-pollinate ideas to improve innovation, ensures that sharing and building on each other's ideas remain positive for the teams and for the company. All these elements facilitate the emergence of collaboration within a team and between teams.

But collaboration requires a combination of mutual support and mutual challenge to achieve positive outcomes and to address change effectively. Mutual support is needed to encourage cooperative approaches and to avoid competitiveness and self-centeredness. Mutual challenge is needed to avoid complacency and to push the team towards breakthrough solutions to problems.

This is best achieved when the team enjoys psychological safety, meaning that team members feel they can take risks without feeling insecure or embarrassed, as found in the 2012-2016 Aristotle study by Google on the effectiveness of teams, conducted on more than 180 Google teams.

The Google findings reinforce another previous study on team effectiveness. In 2008, a group of psychologists from Carnegie Mellon, M.I.T. and Union College designed a study[39] in which they divided 699 participants into small groups and gave them some assignments requiring collaboration. The results of the study highlighted that the factor that distinguished "good" teams from dysfunctional ones was how teammates treated one another. Some elements of group norms could raise a group's collective intelligence, while other elements could hinder the team's efforts, even if, individually, all the members were exceptionally bright.

As the researchers studied the groups, they noticed two behaviors that all the good teams generally shared. The first behavior is known as "equality in distribution of conversational turn-taking", which means that members of a group speak in roughly the same proportion. The second behavior is "average social sensitivity" meaning that people are good at intuiting how others feel from their tone of voice, their expressions, and other

---

39 "Evidence for a Collective Intelligence Factor in the Performance of Human Groups" by Anita Williams Woolley, Christopher F. Chabris, Alex Pentland, Nada Hashmi, Thomas W. Malone, published in *Science* on October 29, 2010.

nonverbal cues. and they understand when someone feels upset or left out. People on the dysfunctional teams, in contrast, scored below average on these traits and showed less sensitivity toward their colleagues.

In psychology, researchers may refer to traits like "conversational turn-taking" and "average social sensitivity" as components of psychological safety – a group culture that the Harvard Business School professor Amy Edmondson defines as a "shared belief held by members of a team that the team is safe for interpersonal risk-taking." Psychological safety is "a sense of confidence that the team will not embarrass, reject or punish someone for speaking up," Edmondson wrote in a study published in 1999: *"It describes a team climate characterized by interpersonal trust and mutual respect in which people are comfortable being themselves."*

Bringing forth collaboration in a group doesn't come naturally, although many teams, if bonded by a certain level of trust and under positive conditions, may enjoy fruitful collaboration relatively frequently. But when the group is under stress or dealing with challenges, collaboration can easily deteriorate into misunderstanding, disconnection, and antagonism. Collaboration stems from the combination of several personal and social skills that team members can develop.

Social sensitivity

One of the basic concepts that associates of an aequal organization need to realize is that when we interact with others, we are like icebergs meeting. If we are not aware of our own iceberg and if we do not take into account that our peers also have their own icebergs, with unmet needs potentially driving reactive responses in ourselves and others, we will get stuck, in the best case, in misunderstandings or, worse, in conflicts.

Whenever something is said or done that hurts us or make us feel vulnerable, we may withdraw from the conversation, avoid sharing our ideas, or we may react aggressively, stubbornly insisting on being right, or hijacking the whole discussion.

Having a commitment to explore our own iceberg and the icebergs of others is the foundation of social sensitivity.

The more we uncover and acknowledge our own iceberg, and especially how the present situation is triggering our quest to

Image 8: Two icebergs, by Nadjeschda Taranzcewski.

fulfill our needs and values, the easier it becomes for others to "see" our intentions and motivations. At the same time, acknowledging that each of us has our own icebergs, with their layers of thoughts, feelings, values, and needs, may allow us to understand how someone else's behavior makes perfect sense from their point of view, considering their drivers. The next time a colleague does something that we don't understand or which upsets us, we can try to see which need they might be trying to protect with their behavior. Are they trying to receive appreciation? Or are they feeling free to self-express themselves? Do they want to regain a sense of control? Are they yearning for novelty and stimulation? Or are they looking for some sense of meaning?

When all members in a team are committed to moving to a new level of mutual understanding and personal growth, then the key interpersonal competences that will make the team invincible are easily developed: listening, giving and receiving feedback & feedforward, collaborative dialogue, action learning, addressing conflict, and coaching others.

Listening

The first, and sometimes the most powerful, way of engaging others in collaboration is to listen to them. A person who feels listened to – completely, genuinely, with interest, and without the listener processing their own agenda in the background – feels respected, cared for, and dignified. They perceive that the listener really values what they have to say and it empowers them, giving them the authority to speak on and to speak honestly.

It is not an easy task. It requires a genuine desire to connect and understand the speaker's point of view, to set aside the need to affirm one's own ideas, and to concentrate attention on one person with a certain intensity. It's easier to shift to talking and telling, moving the subject to topics that we are more comfortable with and knowledgeable about. We generally search for an opening to give the speaker our own view or experience and when we do that, we are giving them the message that the speaker, and what they are talking about, have no importance.

The power of deep listening brings forth powerful speaking. If we listen with full attention and presence, others thus become more aware of what they are saying – and will, as a result, become more discriminating in their speaking. It is as though we increase the amplification on their speaker system. They may well find themselves saying things they have never said before – or even thought before.

We can train ourselves to listen more deeply, more powerfully to others and in order to do that we need to listen to our own listening. This means becoming aware of the quality of our own listening; acknowledging if we are filtering another's speaking through our own filters, world view, opinions, beliefs, emotional cloud, and cultural screen; and switching to listening without judgment, being fully present and open-hearted.

Offering feedback & feedforward

Feedback and feedforward are essential elements of learning, growing, and changing, on top of being an important ingredient of performance. They give us information about how others perceive us and our level of performance, which areas are considered strengths and which are still to be developed, what we can change to get better results, what needs to happen in our working relationships to strengthen them and make them work better, and how we can be more successful at something.

In an organization of peers, one of the most valuable contributions anyone can make to another person's learning is to offer input on how they are contributing to the team and the organization. Taking the time and energy to offer another person feedback about their work indicates that the feedback giver cares about the receiver and that the receiver's work is worth attention. Feedback and feedforward are gifts shared with the purpose of helping the development of others.

Feedforward, as previously shared, is about giving suggestions for the future, and is by its very nature solution-oriented, future-oriented, non-judgmental, and not something to be taken personally.

Feedback, instead, is focused on past behaviors, and while positive feedback when given on specific observable behavior is always motivating and reinforces self-efficacy, the way negative feedback is presented can be perceived as unhelpful and potentially harmful. Bad feedback makes the receiver feel invalidated as a person. It stems more often from the need of the giver to criticize and judge than from the need of the person receiving it.

Useful feedback, in contrast, shows that the giver values and supports the receiver, and at the same time offers reactions to specific behaviors. Any negative feedback should be raised in an overall supportive context in which the parties can trust one another. The giver's intentions, the tone, and the choice of wording make the difference between bad and useful feedback.

If we say to a peer, "Last night your irritated reaction (our interpretation of your feelings) showed me that you don't care about listening to me (my guess)," we are judging our colleague and trying to blame her. This normally shuts down the conversation or creates a bad feeling.

If we say instead: "Last night, during our meeting, you suddenly stood up (observable fact) and left the room, slamming the door (observable fact). I got the impression (the effect your behavior had on me) that you were upset and I felt sad that we could not continue the conversation," we offer our colleague an opportunity to explain their intentions and their actions without embarrassing them or putting them in the wrong. Maybe they got up and left because they remembered they had forgotten to send a crucial email within a certain deadline and needed to send it right away. We will never know what goes on in somebody else's iceberg, until we ask them and find out.

Collaborative dialogue

When a group of people comes together to, for example, address a problem or to decide the approach to take toward a new challenge, more often than not they have a discussion. The word "discussion" comes from the Latin "discutere", to shake or shatter, as in to shake up ideas or points of view one by one – to discern what is right and what is wrong. We need discussions to determine and decide the rational side of our work. The word "dialogue", however, comes from the Greek word dialogos. Logos means "word" and dia means "through." But it's more than that. In the most ancient meaning of the word, the root of logos meant "to gather together" and suggested an intimate awareness of the relationships among things in the natural world. In that sense, logos may be best rendered in English as "relationship".

Dialogue can be both a focused and intentional conversation where each participant is equal – even with differing views, both listen and speak – and also a way of being, creating conscious and creative relationships. When we engage in dialogue, we seek to acknowledge and set aside fears, assumptions, and the need to win; we take time to hear different opinions and possibilities. In dialogue, tensions and paradoxes can emerge. They are welcome to emerge because the act of embracing paradoxes gives birth to new ideas: collective wisdom.

William Isaac, the author of Dialogue and the Art of Thinking Together, describes it with these words:

"Dialogue is a conversation in which people think together in relationship. Thinking together implies that you no longer take your own position as final. You relax your grip on certainty and listen to possibilities that result simply from being in relationship with others, possibilities that might not otherwise have occurred. To listen respectfully to others, to cultivate and speak your own voice, to suspend your opinions about others—these bring out the intelligence that lives at the very center of ourselves—the intelligence that exists when we are alert to possibilities around us and thinking freshly." [40]

It is important to clearly understand the distinction between discussion and dialogue and when to use which to get the most value out of a situation. Each situation may require discussion, dialogue or a combination of both.

Action learning

Action learning is a dynamic process that involves a small group of people working to solve challenges and concrete problems and helps them to focus on the problem-solving process and on their operating and interaction modes, to make them more effective. During an action learning session, the group addresses a specific theme with the goal of solving it, while working at the same time on the team's ability to work and interact effectively. The action learning application can be limited to specific meetings or used for protracted initiatives over time, depending on the nature of the challenge or problem to be resolved. The focus remains on the "presenter", the person who has the responsibility

---

40 *Dialogue: The Art Of Thinking Together* by William Isaacs, Crown Business 2008.

of the problem to be solved.

Action learning tackles problems through a process of first asking questions to clarify the exact nature of the problem, reflecting and identifying possible solutions, and only then taking action. Questions build group dialogue and cohesiveness, generate innovative and systems thinking, and enhance learning results.

Generally, the group takes advantage of the support of a coach, who is responsible for promoting and facilitating learning as well as encouraging the team to be self-managing. In addition, the learning acquired by working on complex, critical, and urgent problems that have no currently acceptable solutions can be applied by individuals, teams, and organizations to other situations.

The theory of action learning and the epistemological position were developed originally by Reg Revans (1982), who applied the method to support organizational and business development, problem solving, and improvement. It was then popularized by Michael J. Marquardt, professor of Human Resource Development and International Affairs at George Washington University. He developed a model of six components and two ground rules that has gained wide-spread acceptance.

Addressing conflict

Our approach to conflict is that when people are committed to exploring their icebergs and make a conscious effort to communicate their thoughts, feelings, and needs in a constructive and creative way, they do not undergo conflicts, but only experiences that lead to personal growth.

The evolution of conflict has predictable steps, although the process can start anywhere:

- **Discomfort:** Things don't feel right, even though nothing has been said. We are not sure what the problem is, but we feel uncomfortable.

- **Incident:** A short, sharp exchange occurs; our only lasting internal reaction is irritation.
- **Misunderstanding:** Motives and facts are confused or misperceived. We keep thinking back to the problem.
- **Tension:** Relationships are weighed down by negative attitudes. We find the relationship has become a source of worry or concern.
- **Conflict:** Behavior is affected, normal functioning becomes difficult – often resulting in a major event. We contemplate, or even execute, extreme behavior.

Conflicts arise because we do not explore why a certain situation makes us think and feel uncomfortable at the moment that the situation occurs. We avoid looking for the trigger that makes us feel upset and we do not connect the dots between the trigger and our needs, values, or desires. And because we are not aware of what is happening and why it is happening inside us, we are unable to openly and sincerely communicate in a way that the other can understand. It is so much easier to blame, put down, criticize, or diagnose others for what they make us feel. When we judge others, we increase the defensiveness and resistance on their part. If they agree with our analysis of their wrongness, they likely do so out of fear, guilt, or shame.

Another way we feed the escalation of the conflict is when we deny our personal responsibility. We are each responsible for our own thoughts, feelings, and actions. When we say something like: "You make me feel unheard" we deny our personal responsibility for our own feelings and thoughts.

When we imply that other people's behaviors are the cause of our feelings, we disrupt our relationships. The cause of our feelings is never the other person's behavior, it's our needs. It's not what other people do that can hurt us: it's how we interpret it.

The way most of us were educated by parents, teachers, and

caretakers was guilt-inducing, in order to get us to do what they wanted and to make us feel responsible for their feelings. We should not do the same with other people, least of all with our co-workers.

When we express our feelings it is important that we make it clear that the cause behind them is our own needs. And it is also important that we learn to distinguish interpretations from feelings.

Happy, sad, worried, upset, frustrated, curious, and surprised are all feelings. Abandoned, neglected, manipulated, unheard, rejected, misunderstood, and attacked are instead all examples of interpretations. We can easily recognize interpretations because, contrary to the feelings that describe a sensation we have, they imply that there must be someone or something to blame.

The other half of the process in addressing conflict is how we respond to other people's communications. Too often, we tend to give advice, reassurance, and consolation or to explain our own position or feelings. When we do this, we disempower ourselves and others. The best way to listen to others trying to deal with something upsetting them is to show empathy. Empathy is a deep and respectful understanding of what others are experiencing. It means emptying the mind and being fully present with the feelings and needs the person is experiencing in that moment.

In the words of Marshall B. Rosenberg, PhD, author of the book Nonviolent Communication – A Language of Compassion:

"When two disputing parties have each had an opportunity to fully express what they are observing, feeling, needing, and requesting – and each has empathized with the other – a resolution can usually be reached that meets the needs of both sides. At the very least, the two can agree, in goodwill, to disagree." [41]

---

[41] *Nonviolent Communication: A Language of Life*, by Marshall B. Rosenberg, PuddleDancer Press 2005 (p. 161).

Coaching

Coaching is a partnership between a coach and an individual (coachee) or a group, where both parties are engaged in a creative and explorative conversation with the aim of developing individual and team potential and reaching specific objectives.

A coach helps another person or a team to change themselves and to reshape their way of being, thinking, and acting. The coach challenges and supports coachees to achieve high levels of performance and at the same time to bring out the best in themselves.

Coaching's only focus is the coachee. The coach is just a mirror, a sounding board, a thinking partner. This is the fundamental difference between coaching and other disciplines like training, consultancy, or mentoring, in which an expert enables the growth of the other person through the transfer of knowledge, solutions, directives, or lessons. Coach and coachee are like partners, equally contributing to the conversation, and they both grow through the process.

The focus of any coaching conversation is determined by the coachee, who takes responsibility for the results they want to achieve through the coaching process. Through conversations, coaches typically strive to foster new perspectives and insights and to support coachees toward goal-related action commitments.

While at the beginning, coaching inside organizations developed as a paid service provided by an external coach to a client, it evolved in different directions. Robert Hargrove (1995), author of the book Masterful Coaching, positioned coaching as a new form of management focusing on the empowerment of people – and, as such, it was presented as a managerial skill. In the last 15 years, the utilization of coaching in organizations has diversified through:

- External professional coaches who work mainly with directors, executives, and top teams;

- Internal professional coaches who are employees of the organization and provide coaching to teams and front-line employees up to middle managers, either full-time or part-time;
- Managers trained as coaches, who use coaching skills to support the professional development and goal achievement of their subordinates, while remaining cognizant that they have a vested interest in the results of their coachee and for this reason cannot be a full partner in the process like an external coach can.

In AEquacy, coaching goes beyond an activity to perform once in a while or when useful, but becomes a way to relate to each other and to take care of each other's development. Learning to coach others brings great satisfaction and is a mental, rather than a technical, attitude. In a situation where associates are constantly faced with complex circumstances and decisions, coaching has a strong and valuable contribution to offer.

In AEquacy, basic coaching skills are to be learned by all associates, as in each team there is the rotating role of Coach that must be filled by one of the team members. The Team Coach has the responsibility to focus on the team's development; to surface the team's dynamics, both positive and dysfunctional, and guide the team to explore them; to support the team in giving and receiving feedback and feedforward individually and as a group; to preserve the team's purpose; to facilitate the governance meetings (and the operational meetings if needed); and to help individuals and the entire team take ownership of their commitment and responsibilities.

When every member of an organization learns the coaching approach and principles in addition to basic coaching skills, and when they commit to engaging in conversations with a coaching attitude, the organizational culture naturally becomes more resilient, change-oriented, and self-transforming.

Team management

Besides developing personal and interpersonal skills, associates of an aequal organization must familiarize themselves with and become experts on a set of team management practices that relate to both governing the team processes and managing projects in this particular environment.

From the team purpose to the Team Charter

Once a new team comes into being, it is assigned a purpose from the team of peers that created it. The creator can be any other team: Operational, Coordinating, Service, or Source Team. The purpose is a vivid and inspiring description that defines the reason for the existence of the team, including its context: the problem it's trying to solve or the opportunity it's going to chase, the consequences of the problem/opportunity going unaddressed, and the relation of the team to the larger organizational purpose. The purpose clarifies why the group comes together and helps the team make decisions based on what action will move the team closer toward its goals. The first decision that the team is then asked to agree upon is a Team Charter. In a foundational governance meeting, the team discusses all the elements constituting the Team Charter, such as:

OKRs (Objectives and Key Results) and the **strategy** the team is focused on. The strategy is dynamic and subject to regular updates, depending on the market conditions, technological changes, or evolving customer needs and expectations. The team proposes their Key Results, or the metrics the team will use to measure its accomplishments. This part of the document defines how success will look and how the team is going to measure it. It includes conversations and agreements on the desired outcomes of individual team members and how they will they be measured.

Roles needed in the team and their description, together with the **scope** and **accountabilities** linked to each role, including the elective roles of Coach, Meeting Host, and the Connectors. Here the conversation may include potential gaps in the mix of competences of the existing team members and the need to develop them or to recruit new associates from within or from outside the organization. Each person can have more than one role, depending on their skills, natural inclination, and interest.

Budget and resources. The budget can be assigned by the Source Team or generated by the team itself utilizing existing market data and internal budget guidelines. In this conversation, compensations and potential bonuses for each team member need to be discussed and agreed upon.

Team and team members assessment. In this part of the conversation, the team reflects on how both team and team members will be evaluated, when and by whom, provided that comprehensive assessments are to be made by both the internal members and a group of peers outside the team (each member can pick peers from the Coordination Team, the Source Team, or a specific Assessment Team, should the organization decide to appoint one).

The context for all the decisions related to the Team Charter is the Governance Meeting and all the guidelines should be submitted to the creator of the team for further input before being published in the organizational repository or log.

The Team Charter is a dynamic document: the team periodically revises it depending on changing conditions or the evolution of the team's direction.

Defining roles

One of the main decisions that a team should make at the start is the definition and assignment of roles. In an aequal organization there are no jobs or titles that put people in the boxes of an organizational chart. Each associate takes on one or more roles, depending on their skills, experience and interests. In Asterys, for example, Giovanna fills the roles of "marketing master", "program designer", and "senior facilitator".

In contrast to job descriptions that are mostly rigid and go unquestioned (and forgotten) for a long time, in AEquacy roles are dynamic: they evolve according to the situation, the customers' changing needs, or new team guidelines. Because they make it clear for anyone in the organization which person has the authority for a particular project or task, roles are an important reference for everyday activities.

A description of a role includes:

- The name or definition of the role;
- A purpose, or the reason why the role is in place;
- A scope, or the extension of the area for which the person has full authority that cannot be infringed by others;
- One or more accountabilities, or specific activities the person shall perform to fulfill their role.

The roles once assigned to managers in traditional hierarchical companies – such as recruiting, onboarding, planning, assessing team members' performance, monitoring team metrics, addressing conflict, and strategizing – are all distributed among team members.

The process of defining and assigning roles can be addressed in one of the team's governance meetings: the team member who senses that the team needs a new role makes a proposal and the Coach facilitates a round where team members either vote for a colleague who volunteered to take on the role or cast a ballot for who they think should do it.

For complex roles that require a candidate with broader experience or specific skills or when there is a need to recruit from other areas of the organization or from outside, the allocation of the role can be more formal and include a round of interviews of the candidates by those who will be working closely with them, a formal election process (see next paragraph), or a peer-advice process.

Elective roles

Elections are required for the roles of Coach, Meeting Host, and Connectors. The elective roles are all rotating ones and the candidate is expected to fill the role for a limited period, after which new elections must take place. We suggest keeping the process as simple as possible. One way to run team elections is the following:[42]

a) Role description: the Coach presents the role and responsibility that needs to be filled, together with the desired skills and experience or qualities looked for (all those elements would have been approved in an earlier Governance Meeting).

b) Nominations: each team member nominates a desired candidate. Alternatively a team member can decide to pass or to suggest hiring from outside the organization. A nomination can be written on a post-it together with the top three reasons why the member selected that candidate. The Coach facilitates a round of sharing of the nominations and the reasons why.

c) Gathering input: the Coach invites participants to go around the table and raise questions or add more information, without letting the group engage in debate or discussion.

d) Changing nominee: team members are given an opportunity to change their minds on the nominee and choose a new one based on what they have learnt in the previous round. They should share the reason behind the change. A new post-it with the name of the candidate and reasons why replaces the old one.

e) Nomination: the Coach counts the nominations and

---

42 Adaptation of the Sociocracy Election process.

selects the candidate with the highest number. In the event that there are joint winners, the Coach asks those members who voted for other nominees to cast a second ballot for one of the two winners. There is no need for further discussion.

f) Objection round: the Coach asks if there are valid objections to electing the candidate. He or she allows the members, in turn, to voice their objections without discussion and checks their validity (the candidate is asked last). If there are no objections, the Coach declares the results of the election.

g) Integrating objections: in the event that there are valid objections, the Coach may move to the second winner and facilitate another objection round, or he/she can make an amendment to the role description, followed by another objection round.

Developing guidelines

The team, in its governance process, is tasked with creating the guidelines that regulate how work is done in the group. Guidelines do not need to be created from the beginning and be perfectly crafted. The idea is that whenever an issue or an opportunity arises that calls for a guideline, the team addresses it during a Governance Meeting and consents to a guideline that is good enough to facilitate their work for the time being. The team can still define a time frame to measure and assess the effectiveness of an existing guideline and then propose to amend it or delete it.

The guidelines can be strategic or operational. Strategic guidelines are those that, in the absence of a thoroughly structured strategy – which is common in traditional companies but too binding and unsuited to continuous evolution for aequal organizations – give the team some direction. Examples of strategic guidelines are: the definition of a specific focus in the business of the team; what the team should prioritize between two strategic options (for example "prioritize customer satisfaction over standardization of process"). Operational guidelines are criteria that guide day-to-day tactical decisions regarding projects or tasks (for example "recording the status update of a project item within 24 hours of completion"). All guidelines agreed upon must be recorded in an online repository accessible to the entire company.

Submitting a guideline proposal to a governance meeting can be as simple as having the owner or the proposer articulate the issue or the opportunity, the driver behind it, and what they propose in order to solve the problem or take advantage of the opportunity. This pitch must be concise, comprehensive, have business relevance, and advance the goals or functioning of the team or solve a problem that hinders the team.

When the issue is complex and there is no easy solution, the team can opt for an Action Learning session (see previous paragraph on Collaboration) or for appointing a small group tasked with crafting the case and proposing solutions by collecting input from all relevant contributors and advisors, within and outside the team.

Rounds

A "round" is a simple team facilitation tool that allows everyone to share their opinions without creating a discussion. As the name suggests, for a round to be performed, the group and the Coach should sit or stand in a circle.

Generally in a round, the coach invites one member to speak briefly (it can be the person who raised an issue, or simply the first person on the left or the right of the facilitator). Then, the coach goes around the circle clockwise or counterclockwise so that everyone gets the chance to speak. Simple rules should be shared that limit each intervention to one or two minutes and that discourage other team members from commenting, adding information, or responding to the speaker.

Rounds allow those people who speak less easily in front of others, or are particularly reflective, to feel that their contribution has equal value when it is focused and to the point.

When teams get used to rounds, members show greater ability to listen to understand, because they know that their turn to be heard will come, and they do not need to compete for airing time.

Normally the coach asks a question or suggests a topic and refers to the first person in the round, invites them to speak briefly, and when they are done, moves to the next person and repeats the process. The coach continues until all the members have shared.

Check-Ins

Check-Ins are particular rounds that are normally run at the beginning of a meeting or when there is an issue on the table that is difficult to address and solve. The purpose of the Check-In is to allow each person in a group to express in one word or a short phrase how they're feeling and to answer one or two personal questions. These bits of sharing, that are in no way to be discussed, commented upon, or debated by the coach or other members, are key to helping each speaker be and feel present, and to help their teammates understand what is going on under the iceberg waterline that day.

At Asterys, for example, we often ask these two questions:

- "How are you feeling today?"
- "Is there anything keeping you from being present or that is especially at the front of your mind?"

and then we may add a question about how a particular project is moving forward or what team members learned from a recent experience.

The Check-In can be shortened or extended depending on the time available. It has a lot of benefits: it creates an open environment, helps the team to develop an understanding of where people are coming from, helps each member to be present and leave behind concerns and worries, helps to build relationships, and trains team members to lower their waterline and develop more Emotional Intelligence.

In some marine oil platforms the Check-Ins are used as a safety procedure, as operations on the platform can be dangerous: team members need to know if one of their teammates is feeling nervous or tired, so they can together decide to help him or to change their shifts. In many of our client organizations the Check-Ins are used to make sure everyone is mentally as well as physically present and focused, and to increase collaboration and mutual understanding.

Check-Outs

The Check-Out is a quick round scheduled at the end of a meeting in which team members may briefly share:

- What they are feeling after the meeting;
- How well they think the team worked out their meeting and what can be done differently to be more effective (feedback and feedforward);
- Any other sharing the Coach may suggest for the team to engage in.

Balcony moments

The term "getting on the balcony" is used by Ron Heifetz, Professor at the Harvard Kennedy School of Management, to refer to the competence of taking some distance from the action we are performing or the dynamic of the relationship we are engaged in, and observe what is happening and what is about to emerge. It is a powerful way to stop what we are doing and observe the system we are immersed in and use the input to determine the best course of action, in the moment.

In our professional life we generally spend very little time on the balcony; we tend to be "in the dance" most of the time – that is, busy planning, doing, solving problems, and addressing challenges. When we are in the dance, any incident can easily cause us to fight or flee – making us slaves to our automatic reactions. You might argue that if this happens, we can always get up on the balcony and reflect at a later time, after the incident is over, and correct the consequences of how we reacted. However, reflections on our behavior after the fact rarely constitute a good strategy – particularly because some reactive behaviors cause wounds or conflicts that do not disappear simply because we apologize.

The most effective people have learned to stay in the dance AND on the balcony at the same time. They are able to be in the action and see themselves and the context at the same time.

When team members are able to get on the balcony to reflect on their action while they are taking it, they stop being slaves to their automatic reactions. Also, when teams learn to take a balcony perspective even while dancing, they have the ability to change the course of events.

"Balcony moments" are ways to train teams to get on the balcony, freeze-frame the action, and see all the potentially more effective and constructive paths they can take. They will have the feeling that time expands, while around them everything seems like a still image. They feel they are developing power: the power to choose, from among many possibilities, the one that is most useful and most effective.

Governance Meetings

The governance process of a team has the following objectives:

- Define or amend the purpose of the team;
- Define, modify, or remove the policies that team members adopt;
- Define, modify, or remove roles and responsibilities for each team member;

- Define, modify, or remove team priorities, objectives, and key results or metrics;
- Hold elections for the elected roles (Coach, Connectors – Rep-Link, Tune-Link and Cross-Link – and Meeting Host).

The outputs of the Governance Meetings, together with the overall Guiding Principles, Organizational Purpose, Values, and Team Charter, represent the governance of each team. All the Governance Meeting reports from any team must be accessible to all members of the organization.

The Governance Meetings are held on a regular basis agreed by the team members and scheduled by the Meeting Host; however, the Host may schedule additional Governance Meetings at the request of any team member, communicating the meeting day and time to all team members well in advance.

It is the duty of all team members to participate in the Governance Meeting, as the conversations and decisions taken in that context are intended to benefit and may impact the entire team. The Coach and the Meeting Host shall also take part in the Meeting, as they perform two essential roles in the meeting facilitation.

If the Connectors anticipate that the processing of the issues may have an impact on members of other teams, they may invite one additional person only for the purpose of processing a specific issue. The invited participant becomes a temporary team member for the duration of the Governance Meeting.

If one or more team members do not show up at the Governance Meeting, this is taken to mean that they were given an opportunity to consider the different proposals of the meeting and had no objections to them.

Operational Meetings

The aim of Operational Meetings is to enhance the work and output of the team. They are held periodically at an interval that the team considers ideal (weekly, by-monthly, monthly) and when it is important that the whole team is present to get everyone aligned. The Operational Meetings do not exclude that team members can meet formally or informally to move projects forward.

When teams meet at the Operational Meeting, each team member contributes to the agenda and has the opportunity to share updates, to voice proposals, to make requests to colleagues holding influencing roles, and to offer comments and input to enhance the projects the team is working toward.

We suggest that the meeting include specific steps, after having made sure that all team members are fully present with a proper Check-In:

Metrics updates. In a round, every member shares the updated data related to the metrics assigned to each role he or she holds.

Project updates. We strongly suggest using an online project management app like Dapulse, Trello, Basecamp, or similar to make sure that all team members can access the latest updates on every chunk of any project at any time. It is the team members' responsibility to stay updated on what's going on. For the projects that have strategic priority or move forward at rapid speed, it may be useful for the team member owner of the project to briefly share the most important updates and foreseeable evolutions. Although other team members may ask clarifying questions, the Project Update step of the Operational Meeting is not supposed to be a forum for discussion.

Progress. In this step, team members address emerging opportunities or problems in order to leverage the former and solve the latter to move the projects forward.

There are two situations that may be addressed in a team's Operational Meeting:

1) Tactical issues or opportunities that relate to the dynamics or collaboration between one member and one or more other members of the team (for example, an

associate may ask another associate to speed up a process they have responsibility for, in order to allow him or her enough time to perform their tasks);

2) Strategic issues or opportunities that the team should address as a whole group with everyone participating in the decision-making (for example finding a solution to a changing request from a client that impacts the work of the whole team).

When addressing a tactical issue, the agenda item owner can:

- Request support from another member of the team;
- Request a particular action or behavior from one or more members of the team;
- Propose ideas or solutions to address a problem or to advance a project;
- Request or share information that can advance a project;
- Request help from the team to clarify the issue the proposer would like the team to address.

In facilitating a tactical issue or opportunity, the Coach simply asks the item owner what he or she needs and from whom. The agenda item owner makes the request or proposes an idea to others as needed, and when the team member(s) involved accept the request or the idea, then the outcome is noted in the progress report.

For items that fall into the responsibility of a specific role and for which the associate requests input from the group, there is no need to look for consent from the group, because the agenda item owner has full authority to listen to other team members, and to take a final decision on his or her own.

In facilitating a strategic issue or opportunity, the Coach follows the six steps of consent decision-making that we introduced in Chapter 4 – Smart Systems:

1. Presentation of the issue or idea and the driver;
2. Clarification round;

3. Reactions round;
4. Proposer's response;
5. Objections;
6. Integration.

In both the Governance and Operational Meetings, the agenda items can be developed at the beginning of the meeting by having the Coach go around the team and collect emerging issues or ideas.

The meeting duration should be established beforehand and the team should make the decision to address all items in the time allotted, that is, assigning a time limit to each agenda item, or moving some of the items to a follow-up meeting.

The role of the Coach is key in supporting the agenda item owner to move forward and in preventing team members from diverting the conversation to elements or details that are non-pertinent or non-relevant. If the discussion of an agenda item raises an issue or idea from another team member, the Coach may suggest adding an agenda item to keep the focus on the original item and then support the other team member in addressing his or her own issue or idea.

The Chapter in a nutshell

- In AEquacy there are some key competences, besides technical skills, that all associates should develop in order to optimize the organizational performance and the system dynamics.

- The first set of competences relates to Personal Mastery, or the ability to cultivate self-awareness and to self-regulate one's own mental and emotional states. The idea is to become mindful of one's own reactive patterns and to develop the ability to shift one's mindset and behavior when the pattern doesn't serve a productive outcome.

- Parallel to developing self-awareness comes the development of System Awareness. Sensing the dynamics of the team one belongs to, of the whole organization, and of the dynamics between the latter and its stakeholders is an extremely useful competence which can help one to influence a system where there is no hierarchical power.

- The engine behind AEquacy's superior performance is collaboration. Each associate benefits from learning how to engage in creative conversations, to address conflict productively, and to stay on a path of continuous learning through coaching, feedback, and feedforward.

- The fourth area of competence relates to mastering the ability to self-organize, by maintaining healthy team governance and operations, and by engaging in consent decision-making when useful.

6 - EMBRACING AEQUACY

The situations where AEquacy could be introduced in an organization are generally of two kinds: either the company is a start-up, an organization that is still to be born or has just been created, or the company has been around for a while and already has a more or less ingrained structure, culture, and processes.

The steps for introducing an aequal structure don't really differ that much in the two contexts. In the former situation the adoption of AEquacy is often facilitated by the fact that the company is like a blank canvas, with no pre-existing procedures, rules, habits, or beliefs that need to change. In the latter, when the company has been up and running for some time, the introduction of AEquacy transforms not only structures and systems, but also the established ways in which people work, collaborate, relate to each other, and perform, as well as their psychological contract with the organization. In this context the transition process can be seen as an entire system change, demanding higher levels of complexity in comparison to the first scenario.

In this Chapter we will take a look at what are, in our experience, the most effective steps for implementing AEquacy in an organization, whether a start-up or an established company – bearing in mind that in the latter situation, change management requires extra effort, energy, time, and care to enable the employees (or the majority of them) to transition to and embrace a new mindset and what is, for them, a revolutionary operating system.

The pitfalls of change management

The existing data on the success rate of change efforts is limited and sometimes anecdotal, but all the estimates come to similar conclusions: bringing about organizational change successfully is a tough job. In 1993, Michael Hammer and James Champy, authors of the book Reengineering the Corporation remarked: *"Our unscientific estimate is that as many as 50 percent to 70 percent of the organizations that undertake a reengineering effort do not achieve the dramatic results they intended."*

In a 2000 Harvard Business Review article, co-authors Nitin Nohria and Michael Beer observed: *"Change remains difficult to pull off, and few companies manage the process as well as they would like. Most of their initiatives—installing new technology, downsizing, restructuring, or trying to change corporate culture—have had low success rates. The brutal fact is that about 70% of all change initiatives fail."*

In 2008 John Kotter shared his own estimate for such failures in his book A Sense of Urgency and wrote that more than 70 percent of change efforts either fail to be launched, fail to be completed, or finish over budget.

The 70% failure rate has been cited in hundreds of articles and books about change management, even though this number emerged only from the personal observations of those consultants, not as a product of well-crafted research.

Finally, in 2009, McKinsey published the result of a survey[43] of

---

43 *The Inconvenient Truth about Change Management* by Scott Keller and Carolyn Aiken (http://projektmanazer.cz/kurz/soubory/modul-c/the-inconvenient-truth-about-change-

1,546 business executives from different countries that highlighted that only 30% of the sample agreed that their change program had been "completely/mostly successful".

The issue of resistance to change

When we look at the reasons why change programs fail to achieve target impact, a 2008 study by McKinsey & Company[44] revealed that the two most important factors in failure are:

- Employees are resistant to change (39%); and
- Management behavior does not support change (33%).

The other two more marginal factors are inadequate resources or budget (14%) and other obstacles (14%).

In the last twenty years the majority of consultants, Human Resources professionals, and Organizational Development specialists have planned and executed change programs anticipating that at some point they will have to deal with resistance to change. The smartest of them have begun to include the transformation of people's mindsets and behavior in their change programs.

One of the most successful change models was created by McKinsey and is called the Influence Model.[45] Since its release, it has had a major impact on how change programs are carried out. It has four components, all of which – McKinsey suggests – should be in place to ensure that change occurs and lasts: fostering understanding and conviction; reinforcing changes through formal mechanisms; developing talent and skills; and role modeling.

The basic idea is that "employees will alter their mindsets only if they see the point of the change and agree with it—at least enough to give it a try. The surrounding structures (reward and

---

management.pdf).

44 Beer and Nohria (2000); Cameron and Quinn (1997); CSC Index; Caldewell (1994); Gross et al. (1993); Kotter and Heskett (1992); Hickings (1988); Conference Board report (Fortune 500 interviews); press analysis; McKinsey analysis.

45 "The psychology of change management" by Emily Lawson and Colin Price, *McKinsey Quarterly*, June 2003.

recognition systems, for example) must be in tune with the new behavior. Employees must have the skills to do what it requires. Finally, they must see people they respect modeling it actively. Each of these conditions is realized independently; together they add up to a way of changing the behavior of people in organizations by changing attitudes about what can and should happen at work."

Many change models are focused on pushing the change from the top by persuading staff through heavily and repeatedly communicated compelling change stories; on convincing a group of managers to become internal supporters (what Kotter defines as "a guiding coalition") who buy into the change plan in order to influence other employees and mitigate resistance; on communicating repeatedly about the change; and on training staff to accept the change. And all of this with the aim of reducing resistance.

It is interesting to note that the idea of employees' resistance to change is not an objective reality. As quantum physics teaches us, there is no objective reality out there: reality is only subjective and depends on the observer and on expectations, beliefs, and mindsets. Thus, in the available research about why change fails, the resistance of employees is but one perspective reported by change agents and biased by their expectations and their interpretation of the change recipients' behaviors.

Let us introduce the definition of change agent. What we mean by change agent is any corporate leader, change consultant, or appointed change catalyst inside an organization who is in charge or involved in designing and/or implementing change.

Change agents are generally portrayed as facing an irrational and dysfunctional response on the part of change recipients,[46] without taking into consideration that agents are active participants in and co-creators of the change outcomes with their

---

46 "Resistance to Change: The Rest of the Story," by Jeffrey D. Ford, Laurie W. Ford and Angelo D'Amelio, *Academy of Management Review* 2008, Vol. 33, No. 2, 362-377.

own behaviors and communication.

In 2009-2010 twenty facilitators from Asterys were involved in a large change program impacting over 5,000 branch directors of one of the most important banks in Italy. We worked in collaboration with a leading consulting firm, which was assisting the bank with changing processes and systems, while our facilitators were brought in to support the branch directors in making sense of the changed role awaiting them. Our session followed a two-day workshop delivered by the consulting firm on more technical issues and each morning before entering the meeting room, the consulting firm trainer would provide a brief onboarding so that the Asterys facilitators could get a sense of what had happened up to that point. The most common advice we kept hearing every single morning in these onboarding sessions was that a certain number of branch directors in the group were resistant and cynical, as they had been through many other ineffective change programs before and it was hard to press the message of the change without producing discussions, sarcastic comments, and push-backs. The change agents therefore diagnosed a certain level of "resistance to change" that would affect the program and suggested that we should address such resistance in our sessions. Our preference, on the other hand, has been to engage workshop participants in open and non-judgmental conversations about workshop participants' hopes, concerns, and feelings and to provide them with tools to develop a better understanding of what was going on inside themselves and how they could regain confidence during the change process. And, to the surprise of the consulting firm's trainers, every single evening the group of directors ended up inspired, empowered, and engaged. Where had the resistance gone?

The fact is that when change agents receive questions, doubts, sarcasm, and alternative solutions as a reaction to their change messages, they tend to label people's reactions as "resistance" instead of considering them as a form of energy that can fuel the change and maintain momentum and as a form of feedback on their (ineffective) ways of pushing change forward. Generally speaking, change agents do not consider that in most cases they contribute with their own actions and decisions to:

Breaches of existing agreements and, consequently, loss of trust

This happens every time change agents renege on a promise, an expected behavior, or practice, or modify the allocation of resources following a less than transparent process. When employees perceive injustice or betrayal, they are likely to feel resentment, a sense of being victimized, and a desire to punish the betrayers, along with a loss of trust in their employer.

Breakdowns in communication

This may happen for different reasons. The most common are a lack of or weak communication about the reason for the change (the benefits that change brings to the organization and to the various stakeholders) and the effort to provide rational justifications in response to the greater scrutiny of employees. It may also occur when change agents, intentionally or not, misrepresent the benefits, costs, or success of the change program.

Resistance to resistance

Very often change agents are resistant to ideas, proposals, and counteroffers suggested by change recipients. When exploring with the management teams of large clients how to announce or communicate the change to employees, our proposal to create a forum or a safe space where employees can share their concerns and ideas is too often discarded because the management fears that this would open a can of worms that would question the well-packed and immutable set of changes determined by the few at the top.

We have been involved in designing and delivering change programs for large multinationals since 2004 and we have often applied the ideas behind McKinsey's Influence Model regarding transformation of mindset and behaviors. Moreover, as executive coaches and facilitators we are very experienced at working with participants' emotions, beliefs, needs, and fears at a deep level.

We firmly believe in the power of moving people away from fear and resistance toward finding their own purpose in the change proposed, embracing the challenges that change brings and using these challenges to grow and expand their effectiveness. We totally support the fact that senior leaders and managers have to be good role models for the staff and that systems and processes should be aligned and should support the desired change (although very often this last aspect was beyond our remit in our engagements with our clients and, therefore, often ignored).

Our mindset and behavior transformational programs have always generated incredible feedback and outcomes. Participants feel more in control and more willing to participate in the change effort, they become able to manage and reduce their fears, they feel more empowered, and they renew their enthusiasm.

But too often this new energy and sense of empowerment is not enough by itself to enable the change effort to fully express its potential, especially in the medium and long term. Based on this evidence, we started to question the idea that organizational change failure is due only or mainly to mindset and behaviors, or to an ineffective change management plan.

What was at play that the people leading the change effort didn't see? What could we learn from our experience and how could we make sure that organizations willing to move to AEquacy would increase their chances of success?

A different view of what makes change efforts ineffective

Over the years we have drawn different conclusions as to the real reasons why change efforts do not express their full potential.

The illusion that change works top-down

Like any strategic decision in most organizations, the goals, direction, and process of the change (and often even the tactics) are defined around a small table with very few people. For many multinationals the change goals and strategy come from the parent company and not even the CEO of the specific country has a voice in their definition. In other situations, the CEO sponsors the change, sometimes with the support of the HR department, and with or without external consultants.

Then, as many change methodologies suggest, the CEO develops a "guiding coalition", namely a group of senior leaders – generally the leadership team – and maybe a few high-potentials, who ideally embrace the change and push it downward to the rest of the organization. Those involved often comply with the CEO's expectations in the hope of a promotion or a reward or for gaining more power. Usually there is no participation or input from the employees in the change purpose or strategy. Without any participation in the decisions that will impact their future, it is extremely unlikely that employees feel engaged or take ownership of the change.

Research has shown that when people have a personal stake in an outcome, they are more committed to it, by a factor of almost five to one. In a behavioral experiment conducted in 1975 by Yale Professor Ellen Langer,[47] half the participants were randomly assigned a lottery ticket number while the other half were allowed to come up with their own number and write it on a blank ticket. Before drawing the winning number, the researchers offered to buy back the tickets from the participants. Researchers found that they had to pay at least five times more to those who had chosen their own number. The personal involvement of choosing one's own number made participants more invested in the process and committed to the outcome.

Informing employees of the change without involving them in shaping that change is not enough to mobilize their energy; it doesn't give them adequate motivation to go through the difficulties (and sense of loss) of a change.

---

47 "The illusion of control," by Ellen J. Langer, *Journal of Personality and Social Psychology* 1975, Vol. 32.

When management tells people what is changing without seeking any of their input, they miss the opportunity to tap into the energy that comes from the sense that solutions are co-created. This is why coaching is far more effective than any other kind of training or instruction and produces a Return of Investment of 700%[48] – the coach doesn't tell the coachees the answer or the solution to their problems, but helps the coachees to access their own knowledge and wisdom to craft their own solutions. And this not only creates much more accountability and engagement but also more effective outcomes and results.

The illusion that an organization (and its people) works as a machine

At some point, the group of internal change agents in the organization makes sure that some changes are implemented (a new organizational structure, new processes, a re-shuffle of roles and responsibilities, a new IT infrastructure, lean processes, new values and culture, new leadership style, smart working principles, to name just a few).

Management and consultants expect that once the implementation is complete, people automatically change the way they work according to the new rules of the game. Management treats the organization just as a machine. They communicate a set of instructions from the top and expect the machine to be automatically reprogrammed.

They fail to consider the organization holistically, with all the forces and dynamics that can support or hinder the change efforts at both the individual and the organizational level.

Neuroscience helps us to consider how our brain works when we are told what to do. David Rock, a leadership consultant and author of the book Quiet Leadership: Six Steps to Transforming Leadership At Work, and Jeffrey Schwartz, a research scientist at UCLA, maintain that:

---

48 The 2009 International Coach Federation (ICF) Global Coaching Client Study reported the median coaching ROI of coaching to be 700%.

"The traditional command-and-control style of management doesn't lead to permanent changes in behavior. Ordering people to change and them telling them how to do it fires the prefrontal cortex's hair trigger connection to the amygdala. The more you try to convince people that you're right and they're wrong, the more they push back. The brain will try to defend itself from threats."

The illusion that change happens without transformation

Change is what happens in the environment outside of us, above the surface of our reality. It could be a new organizational structure, a new IT infrastructure, a new work methodology. When faced with change, human beings need to adapt and align to the new reality. This adaptation process is called transformation. It happens inside of us and helps us to reformulate how we think, what we believe, and how we feel, so that our consciousness can move past our fears and adapt and embrace the change outside of us.

Transpersonal psychology[49] suggests that the innate desire to develop and grow infuses human beings with energy. Employees will not put sustained effort into a new kind of behavior if they have only an intellectual understanding of why it matters to the company; it must mean something much deeper to them!

If the leadership of an organization does not recognize that there is a need to address the change on one side AND the human transformation on the other, it sets the change up for failure.

What makes our AEquacy implementation model conducive to change

When we started to design the best course of action to support an organization to adopt AEquacy, a few principles were absolutely clear to us, and we built the sequence of

---

49 Transpersonal psychology developed in the 1960s, when Abraham Maslow, Stanislav Grof, and others began integrating the classical Asian traditions of Zen Buddhism, Taoism and yoga into their theories and the practice of humanistic psychology.

implementation phases around those principles:

Broad participation

Contrary to the way most change programs are implemented, with AEquacy all the employees, or a broad representation of them, should be engaged from the beginning in the decisions, in the design and in the planning of the new design. The AEquacy structure and framework of operating principles are not prescriptive. They are like Lego® pieces that each organization can combine in different ways to create customized systems, processes, policies, and organizational culture. We propose the AEquacy concept and the building blocks of the new design to the organization, but employees will design their own company, its purpose, and the way people will work together.

Self-transformation

AEquacy Certified Facilitators are trained to support people to make the shift in consciousness that enables them to update their map of the world, their mindsets, and their ability to move past their fears and embrace change. This support includes a process of alignment between their personal values, what they care about most, and the desired values they want to experience in the organization.

When large numbers of employees go through their personal transformation within a brief time frame, small group by small group, this creates a critical mass of individuals who willingly embrace the new behavior and culture so that both are more likely to be sustained.

Bridging organizational change with people's needs and desires.

Creating a connection between the deeper needs and desires of employees and the higher scope of the change (which should include the meaning of the change for society, for customers, for the company and its stakeholders, for the team, and for the individual employees) can trigger a shift in perspective and behavior. It is important to give change a personal meaning for employees.

Prototyping

The implementation model has been crafted on the principles of Design Thinking. This means that the focus is on an iterative process of:

1. Research – in order to explore potential problems and opportunities for evolving the current AEquacy structure. This phase is human-centered, meaning that it revolves around the AEquacy users, considering the map of stakeholders' needs and desires, and is based on the everyday experience of people.

2. Insights – in order to identify themes and brainstorm solutions and ideas.

3. Ideation – which includes testing the ideas and getting feedback and input to refine the solutions.

4. Experimenting and testing – by implementing ideas and solutions as an early, inexpensive, and scaled-down version, in order to quickly measure the impact and reveal potential problems with the implementation. If problems arise, a new Design Thinking loop is established.

The idea is that any solution is never expected to be definitive and "perfect" from the start, but rather safe enough to try, with cycles of testing and refining until the solution meets the needs of the users.

The AEquacy Implementation Model

The AEquacy Implementation Model we propose has four stages and three steps for each stage.

Staging: In this initial phase, AEquacy is introduced to sponsors and employees to check whether people are ready or willing to embrace AEquacy and whether an aequal design is the solution

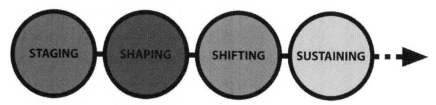

Image 9: AEquacy Implementation Model

that will create value for the specific organization, based on a number of criteria.

Shaping: In this phase all employees, or a broad representation of them, are supported in the co-creation of an aequal structure and the crafting of new systems and processes.

Shifting: The decisions of the Staging phase are implemented and people receive training in Personal and Team Mastery and are supported in their mindset transformation.

Sustaining: In this phase, some activities are planned to maintain the energy needed for completing the shift to AEquacy and to assess potential issues and opportunities to consider in the subsequent evolution.

Although the four stages are implemented in a linear fashion, within each stage some of the steps can have a different order. When it comes to the Sustaining stage, it is not unusual to have loops of evaluating results and iterative improvements.

Let's look in more detail at each step of the four phases.

Staging

Engaging key sponsors: The initial idea to consider the shift to AEquacy originates from one or more members of the organization who are more open to experimenting with new solutions. Oftentimes the idea of a new organizational design comes from the CEO, but it could also originate from the Human Resources or the Organizational Development department, as well as from the leader of a specific department. Whoever decides to consider the idea should start developing allies or sponsors who can support the exploration of the possibility of adopting AEquacy.

Good sponsors are those open to change, those who have demonstrated the ability to pioneer new methodologies or technologies in the past. Sometimes, however, the best sponsors are those who are deeply frustrated with the current situation, who feel the urge and the importance of finding a breakthrough solution to the lack of optimal performance, lack of innovation, bureaucratic slowness, or poor engagement with people.

Assessing readiness/desire to change: The objective of this phase is to introduce AEquacy, its principles, and the new working practices that it enables. Another objective is to allow employees to experiment with how an aequal organization looks and how it differs from the current hierarchical organization. This may include a survey to measure the degree to which employees see AEquacy as a viable organizational design and operating system.

Defining the purpose: Before initiating the change, it is important that the organization shape a new purpose that reflects its higher reason for "being", taking into consideration all stakeholder needs and aspirations, and the different levels of internal and external impact.

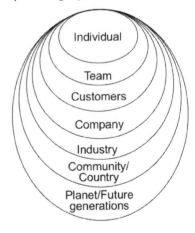

Image 10: Sources of meaning

Creating the context that allows others to make their own connections to what is important to them is critical here. By framing the context, people can make the links between what they do day-to-day and the bigger picture for the business or community as a whole. Some staff may find meaning in knowing how their team contributes to the results of the company or how they solve the customers' problems. Others might find meaning in understanding how what they do helps their business become an industry leader in a particular field, or contributes to the wellbeing of the community or creates better conditions for all people on this planet.

To craft an illuminating and motivating purpose, it's important to start by understanding the diverse and deep sources of meaning of the members of the company.

In companies recently formed and still at an early stage of their development, very often the founders and a group of key employees are those who craft the purpose. In larger organizations, this process bears more fruit if a large group of representatives are charged with crafting the purpose, with the input of the largest possible number of employees.

Shaping

Engaging change catalysts: Once the purpose is clear, defined, and shared by all members, the next step is to invite a group of self-selected associates, who are passionate about making a contribution to the future of their workplace, to craft the organizational map with teams and roles and to suggest the purposes of the new teams. The group of change catalysts will work together in a Project Team and will receive input from all associates who will be impacted by the change of structure.

Co-creating the new design: The Project Team of change catalysts, considering all input from the interested parties, experiments with the components of the AEquacy structure: the Source Team, the Operational and Service Teams, the Coordination Teams and the various roles. The idea, again, is not to make the perfect structure, but to make a structure good enough to be tested and then to keep experimenting and improving.

Agreeing on new systems/processes: The same Project Team that shaped the new organizational aequal structure is responsible for collecting information and input from all the parties affected by the systems and processes that require an adjustment (e.g. to be radically simplified), and for suggesting the system or process change. The new system or process shall be approved by a number of peers coming together in a peer advisory group or the Source Team, depending on the size of the company. The idea is that the decision to adopt a company-wide process or system should not be top-down (and in AEquacy there is no such "top") but peer-based. Some of the processes can be defined at the Operational/Service Team level, or at a Coordination Team level. In this case they can be discussed and agreed upon directly within the team.

Shifting

Transforming mindsets: One of the most effective ways to create a personal transformation is to identify the story or the assumptions we use to give meaning and to interpret what happens around us and within ourselves. These stories or assumptions are only mental constructions, but we treat them as if they were reality, as incontrovertible facts. And we are so unaware of this that we are surprised if others do not agree with us.

These assumptions may be true, but not necessarily so. And in fact, very often they are not. The great advantage of questioning our assumptions is to turn them from being an integral part of us and of our mindset (and therefore invisible to us because we are fully identified with them) into a subject of study and reflection about which we can develop a point of view or perspective, able to see them "outside" of ourselves.

While implementing AEquacy we provide coaching or workshop experiences to the company members that allow them to uncover their limiting mindsets and assumptions and reformulate them so that they can best serve each individual.

Building people capability: A new organizational design and new ways to work and collaborate, as we learned in Chapter 5, require the development of new competences. Learning to access a deeper awareness of self and of the system, develop personal mastery, acquire coaching skills, expand people's ability to connect, collaborate, create psychological safety and trust, and learning how to develop and manage a team are all critical competences for an aequal organization.

Deployment of new systems: The systems and processes agreed upon (at both the organizational level and team level) at this point must be adopted and deployed within the different teams.

Sustaining

Supporting the first steps: It takes a lot of energy to shift from a hierarchical to an aequal organization. On top of the business priorities and expectation of performance, people need to deal with new processes, new jargon, new types of relationship, new responsibilities. It is natural to feel a certain fatigue and energy depletion after a while. In this phase, it can be useful to set up some group or team activities that reignite people with energy, helping them to acknowledge the progress made and to celebrate the first successes.

Some of these activities may include team coaching, retrospectives,[50] World Cafés, or simply appreciating and celebrating each other.

Evaluating results: Some time after the organization has moved to AEquacy, it is useful to make an assessment of the results achieved, around all the key indicators: finance, performance, quality of interactions and collaboration, innovation and the satisfaction and engagement of the associates.

Once the adoption is completed, it's time to detect potential bottlenecks, complications, or problems in order to address and overcome them. Or maybe opportunities for improvement can be identified to strengthen the aequal approach.

The analysis of the problems and opportunities can fuel the

---

50 The term was first used in software engineering, where a retrospective is a meeting to discuss what was successful about a project, what could be improved, and how to incorporate the learning in future iterations or projects. In agile development, retrospectives play a very important role in iterative and incremental development.

next phase.

Iterative improvement loops: following the principles of Design Thinking, an aequal organization is never "done", but evolves over time. Each problem or opportunity to improve emerges from the implementation of the previous step and can spark a new prototype that is tested to determine whether it solves a problem; creates value for associates, customers or stakeholders; or simplifies or improves an existing process.

The benefits of iterative loops of improvement are several:

- They allow costs and people's energy to be conserved, because people don't need to finalize a fully finished solution, but can rapidly test ideas and drafts and get feedback at an early stage.
- They allow early feedback from users to make sure the solution meets user needs.
- They can help associates to adopt changes because they witness the evolution of a solution rather than feeling that a finished solution is simply dumped on them.
- They remind the development team that their efforts are dedicated to adding value for users.
- They allow for easy incorporation of "lessons learned" in the final solution.
- They give stakeholders better visibility of progress at each iteration.

The AEquacy implementation model is co-participative and co-creative in all its steps. This ignites a strong sense of accountability, increases people's ability to manage the new operating system, and generates systems, processes, and an AEquacy structure that is fully geared to the specific people and business needs because there is a broad participation in the creative effort.

The Chapter in a nutshell

- Unless AEquacy is adopted in a newly formed company which has no ingrained culture, beliefs, and habits, the introduction of AEquacy represents a large change management effort.

- All too often change efforts don't reach their full potential, and the research of the last twenty years has identified resistance to change as the main obstacle to successfully implementing change programs.

- Based on our experience, we believe that the real reasons for these pitfalls are: that change plans are decided at the top and imposed on employees; that management acts as if the organization were a machine and that "reprogramming" it is enough to generate the desired change in behavior; and finally, that in the majority of change programs, employees are not supported in making the mindset transformation required to make sense of and embrace the external change.

- The AEquacy implementation model is co-creative and co-participative in nature, and it generates greater accountability and ownership, greater sustainability of results, and higher alignment with the needs of the people and of the business.

- The AEquacy implementation model has four stages. In the Staging stage, AEquacy is introduced to sponsors and employees' readiness to change is assessed. In the Shaping stage employees are supported in the co-creation of the structure, the systems, and the processes. In the Shifting stage, decisions of the previous stages are implemented and people receive training. In the Sustaining phase, the results are measured and problems identified in order to keep the focus on the improvement loop.

ABOUT THE AUTHORS

Giovanna D'Alessio

Giovanna D'Alessio is a Partner at Asterys, an organizational development firm with 100+ Associates in 25 countries. She works as an Executive Coach and Facilitator of Transformation with CEOs, executives, and management teams of large organizations in the areas of culture transformation, change management, conscious leadership, personal effectiveness, interpersonal competencies, and emotional intelligence.

Giovanna is the Director of Asterys Lab's Professional Coaching Mastery training program, accredited ACTP by ICF.

She is currently qualified as a Master Certified Coach. She did her coach training at Coach University, in Colorado and has also studied Emotional Intelligence, personal transformation, Transpersonal Psychology, Systemic Constellations, Voice Dialogue, Design Thinking, and Holacracy.

She founded Federazione Italiana Coach (now ICF Italia, the Italian chapter the International Coach Federation), of which she was the first President in 2002.

From 2004 to 2011 she was a member of the Board of Directors of the International Coach Federation and served as Director-at-Large, Vice President, Secretary/Treasurer, and, in 2010, as President.

Giovanna D'Alessio, MBA, founded and ran a communications agency for 5 years when aged only 20. She then spent 7 years at Saatchi & Saatchi as a Client Director.

From 1998 she worked for Yahoo! Inc. first as the head of the Italian start-up, then in the European headquarters as Marketing Director for Europe.

In 2003 Giovanna wrote the book Come dire No ed essere ancora più apprezzati (How to Say No and Be Even More Appreciated) published by Sperling & Kupfer and in February 2013 RCS Etas published her second book: Il potere di cambiare (the English edition title is Personal Mastery. The Path to Transformative Leadership). In 2016, she was a guest speaker at TEDx (https://www.youtube.com/watch?v=dXdhXCgonIM).

Stefano Petti

Stefano is a Partner at Asterys, a global organizational development firm with 100+ associates in 25 countries and works primarily as thinking partner and executive coach with leaders and managers, largely within multinational contexts, who are engaged in transformational and change initiatives. Stefano is also a passionate international speaker, a lecturer in the Master of International Management program (University of Bologna, Italy) and has been teaching for years in the Executive MBA program (CUOA Business School, Italy).

Prior to entering the areas of organizational and executive development he worked in an international setting and in Italy for Eni Group and Société Générale, with responsibilities that included P&L management, project management of large scale re-organization initiatives, and business development of a start-up.

His academic background includes a university degree in

Business Economics (Italy), a specialization in International Marketing and Finance (Sweden), a Master of Business Administration (London) and master programs in professional coaching (USA). He is certified in using several diagnostic tools in the area of leadership and cultural transformation and in the application of the Organization Workshop and Design Thinking methodologies.

Stefano is an ICF (International Coach Federation) Professional Certified Coach (PCC), former member of the ICF European Leaders Group, former member of the Executive Committee of ICF Italy and co-founder of a non-profit association for the organization of Cultural Events.

He co-authored the Harvard Business Review articles "How Your State of Mind Affects your Performance" (2014), "4 Steps to Dispel a Bad Mood" (2015), "Get in the Right State of Mind for Vacation" (2015) and "A Simple Way to Combat Chronic Stress" (2016). In 2016 Stefano joined the Harvard Business Review Advisory Council.

BIBLIOGRAPHY

Amar A.D., Hentrich C., Hlupic V., "To Be a Better Leader, Give Up Authority," Harvard Business Review, December 2009.

Argyris C., Organizational Traps: Leadership, Culture, Organizational Design, Oxford University Press, 2012.

Argyris C., Integrating the Individual and the Organization, John Wiley & Sons Inc., 1964.

Barrett R., The Values-Driven Organization, Routledge, Abingdon, 2014.

Bingham S., "If Employees Don't Trust You, It's Up to You to Fix It," Harvard Business Review, January 2017.

Brafman O., Beckstrom R.A., The Starfish and the Spider: The Unstoppable Power of Leaderless Organizations, Penguin Group, New York, 2006.

Capra F., Luisi P.L., The Systems View of Life: A Unifying Vision, University Printing House, Cambridge, 2014.

Chamberlain A., Does Company Culture Pay Off? Analyzing Stock Performance of "Best Places to Work" Companies,

Glassdoor Research Studies, March 2015.

Covey S.M.R., Conant D.R., "The Connection Between Employee Trust and Financial Performance," Harvard Business Review, July 2016.

Dirks K., "The Effects of Interpersonal Trust on Work Group Performance," Journal of Applied Psychology 1999, 84 (3): 445-455.

Dvorak N., Nelson B., "Few Employees Believe in their Company's Values," Gallup Business Journal, September 2016.

Dweck C., Mindset: The New Psychology of Success, Random House, New York, 2006.

Feltman C., The Thin Book of Trust, Thin Book Publishing Co., Bend, 2009.

Flamholtz E., "Corporate Culture and the Bottom Line," European Management Journal, Vol. 19, No. 3, Elsevier Science Ltd., Great Britain, 2001.

Foster P.A., The Open Organization: A New Era of Leadership and Organizational Development, Maximum Change Press, Ohio, 2016.

Garvin D.A., Edmondson A.C., Gino F., "Is Yours a Learning Organization," Harvard Business Review, March 2008.

Gray D., The Connected Company, O'Reilly Media, 2014.

Hagel J., Brown J.S., Control vs. Trust: Mastering a different management approach, Deloitte Development LLC, 2009.

Hamel G., "First, Let's Fire All the Managers," Harvard Business Review, December 2011.

Hamel G., The Future of Management, Harvard Business School Press, 2007.

Heifetz R., Leadership Without Easy Answers, Harvard University Press, 1998

Kachaner N., Kunnas P., Always-On Strategy, Boston Consulting Group Publications, April 2017.

Keagan R., Laskow L.L., An Everyone Culture: Becoming a

Deliberately Developmental Organization, Harvard Business Review Press, 2016.

Kirkpatrick D., Beyond Empowerment: The Age of the Self-Managed Organization, Jetlaunch, 2017.

Laloux F., Wilber K., Reinventing Organizations: A Guide to Creating Organizations Inspired by the Next Stage of Human Consciousness, Nelson Parker, 2014.

LeBow R., Spitzer R., Accountability: Freedom and Responsibility without Control, Berrett-Koehler Publishers, 2002.

Lencioni P.M., "Make Your Values Mean Something," Harvard Business Review, July 2002.

Maasik A., Step by Step Guide to OKRS, 2017.

Mackey J., Sisodia R., Conscious Capitalism, with a New Preface by the Authors: Liberating the Heroic Spirit of Business, Harvard Business Review Press, 2013.

Mankins M., Garton E., "How Spotify Balances Employee Autonomy and Accountability," Harvard Business Review, February 2017.

Marciano P.L., Carrots and Sticks Don't Work: Build a Culture of Employee Engagement with the Principles of RESPECT, McGraw-Hill Books, 2010.

Morieux Y., Tollman P., Six Simple Rules: How to Manage Complexity without Getting Complicated, Harvard Business Review Press, 2014.

Moskowitz M., Levering R., "The Best Employers in the U.S. Say their Greatest Tool is Culture," Fortune Magazine, March 2015.

Nielsen, J., The Myth of Leadership. Creating Leaderless Organizations, Davies-Black Publishing, California, 2004.

Oshry B., Leading Systems, Berrett-Koehler Publishers Inc., San Francisco, 1999.

Oshry B., Seeing Systems – Unlocking the Mysteries of Organizational Life, Berrett-Koehler Publishers Inc., San Francisco, 2007.

Pink D., Drive: The Surprising Truth About What Motivates Us, Canongate Books, Edinburgh, 2011

Perlow L.A., Hadley C.N., Eun E., "Stop the Meeting Madness," Harvard Business Review, July-August 2017.

Pflaeging N., Organize for Complexity: How to Get Life Back into Work to Build the High-Performance Organization, Lightning Source Inc., 2014.

Robertson B.J., Holacracy: The New Management System for a Rapidly Changing World, Henri Holt & Co., 2015.

Senge P.M., The Fifth Discipline: The Art & Practice of The Learning Organization, Crown Business, 1990, 2006.

Sisodia R.S., Wolfe D.B., Sheth J.N., Firms of Endearment: How World-Class Companies Profit from Passion and Purpose, Wharton School Publishing, 2007.

Sull D., Homkes R., Sull C., "Why Strategy Execution Unravels—and What to Do About It," Harvard Business Review, March 2015.

White R., "Do Employees Act Like They Think? Exploring the Dichotomy Between Moral Judgment and Ethical Behavior," Public Administration Quarterly, Vol. 25, No. 4 (Winter, 2002), pp. 391-412.

Wodtke C., Radical Focus: Achieving Your Most Important Goals with Objectives and Key Results, Cucina Media LLC, 2016.

Surveys and research

2017 Edelman Trust Barometer Global Report, Edelman, 2017.

Cisco Collaboration Work Practice Study, Cisco Systems Inc., March 2013.

"Corporate Culture – The View from the Top, and the Bottom," The Economist, New York, September 2011.

Edmonson A., "Psychological Safety and Learning Behavior in Work Teams," Administrative Science Quarterly 1999, 44: 350-383.

"Getting Ready for the Future of Work," McKinsey Quarterly,

September 2017.

Global Generation Survey, EYGM, 2015.

Ford J., Ford L., D'Amelio A., "Resistance to Change: The Rest of the Story," Academy of Management Review 2008, Vol. 33, No. 2, 362-377.

The How Report, LRN, 2016.

The New Organization: Different by Design, Deloitte 2016.

Articles and posts

Ashkenas R., "Why Accountability Is So Muddled, and How to Un-Muddle It," Harvard Business Review, November 2012.

Basford T., Schaninger B., Viruleg E., "The Science of Organizational Transformations," McKinsey, September 2015.

Basford T., Schaninger B., "The Four Building Blocks of Change," McKinsey Quarterly, April 2016.

Beer M., Finnstrom M., Schrader D., "Why Leadership Training Fails – and What to Do About it," Harvard Business Review, October 2016.

Burkus D., "Why Being Transparent About Pay Is Good for Business," The Wall Street Journal, 30 May 2016.

Covey S., Conant D., "The Connection Between Employee Trust and Financial Performance," Harvard Business Review, July 2016.

Eisenstat R., Spector B., Beer M., "Why Change Programs Don't Produce Change," Harvard Business Review, November–December 1990.

Jacquemont D., Maor D., Reich A., "How to Beat the Transformation Odds," McKinsey, April 2015.

Keller S., Aiken C., "The Irrational Side of Change Management," McKinsey Quarterly, April 2009.

Mankins M., Garton E., "How Spotify Balances Employee Autonomy and Accountability," Harvard Business Review, February 2017.

70823909R00146

Made in the USA
Middletown, DE
28 September 2019